STAND OUT

STRATEGY
REPUTATION
VISUALITY
AUTHENTICITY
IDEAL LEADS

OLS TO MASTER THE 8 FUNDAMENTALS OF STANDING OUT IN BUSINESS

DISTINCTION
PURPOSE
MINDSET

www.TwinEngine.com

🔠 TwinEngine™

Published by TwinEngine, Houston, Texas

For requests to the publisher for permission or more information:
TwinEngine
7650 San Felipe, Houston, Texas 77063
www.TwinEngine.com
713-255-1370
StandOut@TwinEngine.com

ISBN 978-0-9968389-0-0

Printed in the United States of America
First Edition

FOR JAMES

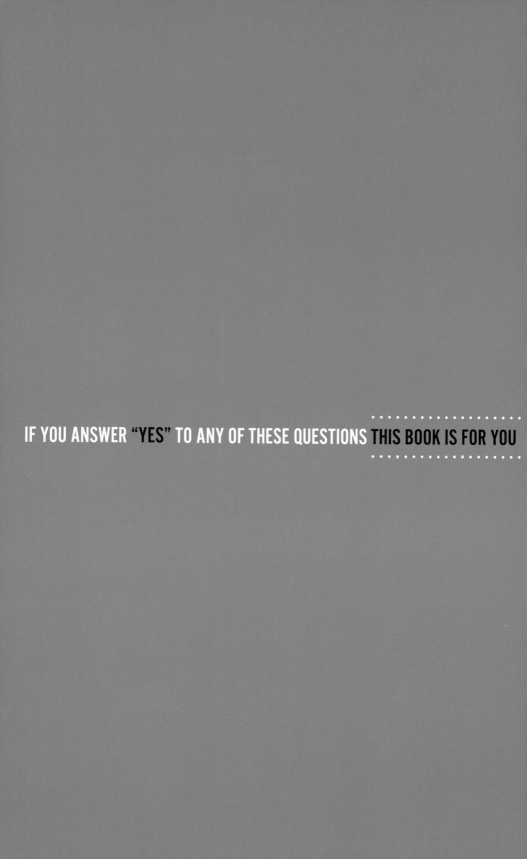

IF YOU ANSWER "YES" TO ANY OF THESE QUESTIONS THIS BOOK IS FOR YOU

HAS THE COMPETITIVE LANDSCAPE MADE IT HARDER AND HARDER TO STAND OUT AMONG COMPETITORS AND GET NOTICED? DO YOU WANT TO KNOW WHAT MAKES YOUR BUSINESS TRULY DISTINCT SO IT STANDS OUT? DO YOU FEEL LIKE YOU ARE MISSING OUT ON OPPORTUNITIES?

THIS BOOK IS DIVIDED BY THE FUNDAMENTALS.

YOU CAN READ FROM START TO FINISH OR

JUMP TO THE FUNDAMENTAL YOU NEED TO STRENGTHEN.

STAND OUT:

THE 8 FUNDAMENTALS:

INTRODUCTION

THE IMPORTANCE OF STANDING OUT IN BUSINESS

You may have a solid business strategy and plan, an excellent product or service, talented and dedicated employees and a rockstar sales and marketing team—you may be doing all these things right, but if you don't stand out, you lose.

Today, we're bombarded with marketing messages from every side—the *New York Times* estimated that a person living 30 years ago saw up to 2,000 ad messages a day, compared to over 5,000 messages today. Marketers used to try to reach consumers at home watching TV or reading newspapers and magazines, but now advertisers reach consumers in real time, trying to catch their attention at every turn. It's absolute sensory overload as companies press harder to make their brands stand out.

Yet, a familiar and trusted brand still has the ability to cut through the clutter—especially when a prospect needs the product or service that it offers. The obvious question is: How does a brand become "familiar and trusted?" And for emerging businesses, how can they stand out from their competitors in a way that people learn to know and trust them?

This book offers a new perspective and a clear and structured approach to mastering how to stand out, be remembered, and become a trusted and preferred choice of customers and prospects. We will do this by focusing on the eight fundamental areas of a brand: purpose, reputation, visuality, authenticity, ideal leads, distinction, strategy and mindset.

You will find diagnostic assessments and exercises which will identify your distinct advantage—those talents, qualities and values that define who you are as an individual and as a business—and show you how to leverage them to Stand Out.

At TwinEngine we've worked with brands for over two decades who thought that the next flashy advertising campaign would take them to the next level. But the simplest formula for sustaining business growth, building brand equity and standing out is to be more of who or what you already are. And to do it truthfully and authentically. Why? Because authenticity is sustainable and it sells.

Customers recognize and value honesty, simplicity and integrity. They are attracted to it and will generally pay more to have it. When you're not authentic, customers can tell. And in today's online, real-time environment, if you don't tell the truth, someone else surely will. Customers also value clarity. They want to know what it is about you and your business that is different and truly unique.

My sister, Lorrie (co-author of this book), and I are identical twins. Being identical twins, we know a lot about the confusion and frustration that comes from a lack of clarity when things look the same. Until our late teens, we were known as one person "Winnie-Lorrie" (that's one word) or "The Little Twins." It has taught us a simple truth about differences. When you look at identical twins, what do you think? How are they different? What makes each of them unique? Identical twins are intriguing — it's because people can't usually tell them apart.

YOU STAND OUT FROM THE COMPETITION WHEN YOU KNOW YOUR DISTINCT ADVANTAGE.

We live in a world that appreciates and expects individual differences in appearance and behavior. So when we encounter two identical individuals (like Lorrie and myself), this experience challenges our beliefs about the way that the world works.

Of course, identical twins are never exactly alike, and some differ in profound ways. Yet we can't stop ourselves from comparing them and trying to find the differences that help us to tell them apart. By taking a closer look at twins, we can learn a great deal about the concept of differentiation. By looking past what's just intriguing, we can learn about how we perceive differences in anyone or anything.

When I look at my twin, I can experience how others view me—and actually *see myself from outside of myself*.

TO MOST CONSUMERS COMPETING PRODUCTS LOOK ALMOST IDENTICAL

I've learned first hand to identify and appreciate what makes us different. There are physical differences and there are inner differences—one of us is a left-brain thinker and one is a right-brain thinker. One is creative and expressive; the other is rational and linear. But it's the pairing and integration of these different qualities that makes our agency "TwinEngine" what it is. It's our distinct advantage: right brain, left brain, creative and analytic. And when the two work together as one, the whole is greater than the individual parts. From first-hand experience at refining our individuality throughout our lives, we've perfected the ability to perceive distinct differences in other people, other companies and other brands.

TO STAND OUT, YOU NEED TO BE MORE OF WHAT MAKES YOU WHO YOU ARE — THOSE VALUES, PASSIONS, TALENTS, AND EXPERIENCES THAT MAKE YOUR BUSINESS WHAT IT IS — THOSE POSITIVE QUALITIES THAT YOUR CUSTOMERS ALREADY APPRECIATE. YOUR CHALLENGE IS TO IDENTIFY THOSE THINGS AND NURTURE THEM, EXPOSE THEM AND PROMOTE THEM — BECAUSE THEY ARE YOUR DISTINCT ADVANTAGE AND THE SOURCE OF YOUR SUCCESS.

HOW THIS BOOK WILL HELP YOU STAND OUT, TAKE OFF AND STAY ON COURSE

Being more of whom and what you are sounds like a simple idea, but the process of applying this concept to grow your business's bottom line is more complex.

We believe that each of us has a built-in navigation system—an accumulation of all that we've learned—that works like a compass to point us toward our truths (authenticity) and highest potential. Throughout this book we'll talk about the importance of leveraging this to know what's true and what isn't. Truth and authenticity, in the sense that we use those terms here, are largely personal matters. You know better than anyone what's true for you, when you're on course and when you're off. So, as you go through the sections and exercises in how to Stand Out, read with your navigation system turned on. That way you'll feel what's true and relevant for you and take away the parts that will serve your growth.

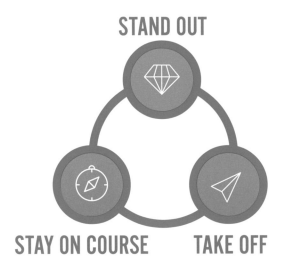

STAND OUT

STAY ON COURSE   **TAKE OFF**

The sections of this book explore The 8 Fundamentals that we've determined in our 25 years of experience are essential to growing your brand and developing its full potential. Though any company can benefit from the information presented here, most of those with whom we work have realized that something is missing or lacking in their strategy. They're working hard, but the gap between where they are and where they want to be isn't shrinking.

This book can change that. The concepts and exercises are specifically structured to uncover what is missing from your business or marketing plan. We have even seen this system of brand alignment provide just the inspiration and momentum a business needed to make a huge leap forward in performance and profitability.

SO, LET'S GET STARTED

Before you can take steps to Stand Out, you need to identify where you are. Our Brand Traffic Control system is designed to do just that. Through a series of diagnostic questions, we'll pinpoint problem areas and uncover opportunities to help focus on what next steps are right for your business—for where you are now and where you want to go.

IDENTIFY YOUR CHALLENGES:
STAND OUT:

- ☐ The competitive landscape is making it hard to stand out
- ☐ We have lost sight of our purpose
- ☐ We don't know our competitive advantages
- ☐ Our visual identity/messaging is weak
- ☐ We don't know who our ideal leads are
- ☐ We don't know our value proposition as a company
- ☐ We don't know what our online reputation is

TAKE OFF:

- ☐ We need a next level strategy
- ☐ We need to target our ideal leads
- ☐ We have stalled and need a plan to take off
- ☐ We need to position as an industry thought leader
- ☐ We need a consistent funnel of qualified ideal leads
- ☐ We need to align business goals and marketing strategies

STAY ON COURSE:

- ☐ We have drifted off course and need to realign
- ☐ We need a plan to measure what works and what doesn't
- ☐ We need to meet regularly to ensure that we are all aligned
- ☐ We need a 12-month marketing plan
- ☐ We need a focused mindset

Challenges Exercise: Utilize this checklist as a team exercise to evaluate what areas need strengthening and to prioritize key initiatives (Each member works on independently, then evaluates together).

IDENTIFY YOUR CHALLENGES:

NUMBER 1 CHALLENGE:

TOP 5 CHALLENGES:

Challenges Summary: After each member works on independently, and you evaluate together, record the collective top 5 challenges and the organization's number 1 challenge.

FROM OUR 25+ YEARS OF EXPERIENCE WE HAVE D

THESE TO BE THE BASIC FUNDAMENTALS WHICH CO

STANDING OUT IN BUSINESS.

BY FOCUSING ON, PRACTICING AND MASTERING THESE FUNDAMENTAL AREAS YOU WILL STAND OUT, TAKE OFF AND STAY ON COURSE.

THE EIGHT

THE 8 FUNDAMENTALS OF STANDING OUT IN BUSINESS.

The order in which The 8 Fundamentals are presented in this book is not necessarily how a company will or should examine them in relation to its operations. Each organization has different strengths and needs and is at a different place, and should work with the fundamentals in the order that best serves its growth.

☐ Purpose ☐ Ideal Leads

☐ Reputation ☐ Distinction

☐ Visuality ☐ Strategy

☐ Authenticity ☐ Mindset

THE 8 FUNDAMENTALS OF STANDING OUT IN BUSINESS

Throughout our 25+ years of experience, we have identified eight primary factors which contribute to standing out from the competition when it comes to marketing. We've distilled what we've learned into The 8 Fundamentals we define below. Ideally this information will help you to shine a light on shortcomings or challenges in your marketing strategy and offer suggestions and solutions for you to Stand Out from the competition, Take Off in a direction that's true to who you are and where you want to be, and, finally, to Stay On Course to reach your goals.

Purpose: The organization knows and lives its purpose, knows what it stands for and is true to its beliefs.

Reputation: There is continuous and ongoing awareness of the organization's reputation and top competitors.

Visuality: The outward appearance of the brand truly reflects who the organization is and the value it delivers.

Authenticity: The organization's messaging is consistent, true, genuine and communicates value propositions.

Ideal Leads: There is a consistent funnel of ideal leads that are defined, nurtured and managed.

Distinction: The organization stands out among its competitors, influencers and industry thought leaders.

Strategy: A 12-month marketing plan is in force and aligned with the organization's goals.

Mindset: There is focus and commitment to achieve desired results.

BRAND TRAFFIC CONTROL

It's a big sky out there—and brand managers can get overwhelmed trying to keep track of how and if their own brand is being noticed and preferred by prospects and customers. How can you know with any certainty if your brand is on course or lost among dozens or even thousands of competitive brands?

Companies can't direct the conversation about their brands in the way they could before online and social media conversations began. Traditional market research has to be combined with active listening and monitoring of what's being said or written about your brand. Today, a dialogue is the solution.

People who like and endorse your company on social media can be important brand ambassadors and make a greater impact on buying decisions than traditional advertising. Your brand is shaped by the public—by the people commenting on or recommending your products and services. But, do you have the tools to influence and direct the conversation?

When you strengthen The 8 Fundamentals, your brand will stand out; you'll know where you are relative to your competition; you'll know how to create consistent messaging to your ideal lead to increase engagement; your brand will be in alignment; you'll be able to execute plans more effectively; you'll know what makes your brand distinct; you'll have a tool to measure what's working and what isn't; and, you'll be able to position your brand to take off.

LOCATE YOUR CURRENT POSITION

In order to determine what you need to do to stand out using the Brand Traffic Control system, you need to know where you currently rate on each of the fundamental brand attributes and how aligned your team is in the perception of where the company stands on each.

BRAND TRAFFIC CONTROL RADAR

This Brand Traffic Control assessment tool graphically plots the current status of The 8 Fundamentals of brand alignment that are key to an organization's success. Using definitions for each fundamental as outlined earlier in this section, consider the current position of your organization within each indicator. Engage each member of the management team to individually complete this assessment and compare your evaluations as a group to assess alignment among the team. Scale: zero in the center (non-existing) to five on the outside ring (highest level). **Go to www. TwinEngine.com/BTC to download the tool.**

· ·

IF YOU DON'T KNOW WHERE YOU ARE GOING, YOU'LL NEVER GET THERE.

· ·

WHAT'S ON YOUR RADAR?

BTC Radar Exercise: Go to www.TwinEngine.com/BTC to download the radar to plot your opinion of the current position of your organization within each indicator on a scale of zero in the center (non-existent) to five on the outside ring (highest level).

BRAND TRAFFIC CONTROL ASSESSMENT

The Brand Traffic Control survey is a more detailed assessment of where your company stands. It includes 12 categories, each with 5 levels, to assess the degree to which a fundamental is being practiced. In addition, there are assessments of additional components of branding, such as Brand Personality, Brand Equity, Brand Standards and Planning.

Get started by asking your team these questions:

- [ ] Do we know and live our purpose as an organization?
- [ ] Do we know what is being said about our brand online?
- [ ] What is our number 1 strategic business goal?
- [ ] How would you describe our organization's personality?
- [ ] What are our value propositions?
- [ ] Who is our ideal lead?
- [ ] How do we stand out?
- [ ] What is our most effective form of marketing?
- [ ] Do our marketing efforts support our business strategy?

The results of this survey indicate which tools may be useful in further defining and strengthening areas showing misalignment. Many of these diagnostic tools are available throughout the sections of this book. **Go to www.TwinEngine.com/BTC to access the survey.**

FIRST, LET'S CLEAR UP AND DEFINE THE MEANING OF "BRAND."

BRANDING TODAY

A brand used to be considered a logo, a slogan, a particular design or color combination, an advertisement or even a brochure. But today, these visual elements are only an outward expression and a small part of what makes up what we recognize as a company's expression of its brand.

A COMPANY'S BRAND IS LIKE A PERSON'S REPUTATION

In today's business environment, a brand is a set of expectations, memories, stories, and relationships that, taken together, account for someone's decision to choose one product or service over another. It's an intangible asset for any company, and possibly the most valuable asset a company owns.

A BRAND IS WHAT YOU ARE

Your brand is comprised of many things that define who you are as a business. These things are mostly intangible—like your purpose for being in business, your reputation, values and beliefs and your unique advantage (the specific qualities and strengths that differentiate your product or service). Add to this mix the emotional impressions and experiences that customers have when interacting with your company and you have an idea of what defines your brand.

SUCCESSFUL BRANDS WILL NEED TO FOCUS ON EMPLOYEES LIVING THE BRAND AND MARKETING FROM THE INSIDE OUT. MARKETING CAN NO LONGER BE A "DEPARTMENT."

MARKETING IS WHAT YOU DO

The tangible, visible things, like your company name, logo, signage, design elements, website and printed materials, are part of your marketing efforts. They are what you do.

Ideally these tangible elements should be an accurate representation of what you are. If these intangible and tangible things align to create an authentic and consistent impression of what you are and what you do, then you have a much greater chance of your business standing out and growing from a good company into a great one.

MAIN TYPES OF BRANDS

There are several different types of brands that you'll recognize in the marketplace today. Here are a few main categories with examples:

Premium Brand—A premium brand focuses on high quality, on limited quantity and exclusivity. Premium brand products typically cost more than other products in the same category. Examples: Mercedes Benz, Rolex, Cartier, Tiffany & Co.

Economy Brand—An economy brand is a brand that places emphasis on easy availability and an affordable price. It is typically marketed based on a very flexible price point and is often subject to sales and specials. It may be used strategically as a means to attract consumers to a business location specifically to encourage add-on sales. Examples: Walmart, Sears, McDonalds.

Corporate Brand—When a company's name is also used as a "product" brand name, this is referred to as corporate branding. Examples: GE, Apple, IBM, Dow, Johnson & Johnson, 3M, VISA.

THE ADVERTISING INDUSTRY TODAY

The traditional, large, multinational advertising agency as portrayed in the television series Mad Men is a thing of the past. The changes in the ad agency world are similar in some ways to changes that have occurred in the music industry. It is adapting and transforming in response to circumstances outside of its control. In the advertising world, the changes are due in part because traditional media spending is giving way more and more to digital and social formats, and partly because the Internet, online and digital have changed the nature of the relevance of scale. Being bigger no longer guarantees strategic excellence or digital aptitude. As the media world has changed, advertising firms are having to adapt to remain competitive with leaner, nimble and more agile smaller specialty agencies. The future will require collaboration and coordination among a diverse group of efficient specialists to deliver the best strategic marketing solutions.

Brands need to know, live and communicate their purpose to differentiate themselves in their marketing efforts. Customers are looking to buy why you sell as much as what you sell. So, you must make "why you sell" an important part of your messaging.

Successful brands will also need to focus on employees living the brand and marketing from the inside out. Marketing can no longer be a department. All employees must be able to communicate the company's mission and vision, becoming, in effect, brand ambassadors.

Brand alignment has become a key corporate initiative. Brand success will require simplification and alignment with core business strategies. Brand alignment will increasingly replace departmentalization and silos in the corporate infrastructure. Integrated marketing will support this shift and will make marketing and branding efforts more effective and strategic.

WHAT'S IN AND WHAT'S OUT

The advertising industry is no stranger to disruption, being one of the first industries transformed by the Internet years ago and currently by the implications of big data. Big changes lead to big opportunities.

WHAT'S IN	WHAT'S OUT
ONE-TO-ONE Targeted to the individual	**MASS MARKETING** Targeted to everyone
REAL HUMANS Human to human	**BOTS** Algorithmic outcomes
LOCAL FOCUS Real-time and where you are	**BROAD FOCUS** Marketing to the masses
DIALOGUE Two-way conversation	**MONOLOGUE** One-way marketing
BEHAVIORAL Understands your needs	**MECHANICAL** Unemotional
SOCIAL PLATFORMS Conversational	**STATIC WEBSITES** Informational
MOBILE In your hand	**DESKTOP** On your desk

ELEVEN ATTRIBUTES OF THE WORLD'S MOST MEMORABLE BRANDS

1. The brand is consistent.

A strong brand maintains a successful balance between continuity and change. A strong brand is consistent with its message of product or service benefits through different promotional campaigns and to varying audiences. It avoids creating confusion or sending conflicting messages about who it is or what it sells.

2. The brand reflects the company's core values.

A company's products and services should be an extension of what a company stands for and believes in, those essential principles that guide its business operations and relationships. Core values help consumers understand a company's personality and build trust in the brand and its products and services.

3. The brand maintains its relevancy over time.

With strong brands, equity is a dynamic attribute. It's tied to the actual quality of a product or service, as well as other intangible aspects that may change over time.

4. The brand uses a full range of marketing and communications activities to build brand equity.

A strong brand uses all of the elements associated with the brand—logos, symbols, slogans, packaging and signage to enhance and reinforce consumer awareness of the brand over time. It uses these elements consistently across multiple media, in advertising, in sales promotions, online, through sponsorships and through endorsements to spread recognition and build awareness of the brand across the marketplace.

5. The brand does an excellent job of delivering the benefits that customers need and desire.

Why do customers buy a product? It's not just because of the product features and attributes, but also because of the brand's image, reputation, quality of service, and several other factors. This unified impression in the consumer's mind is what influences buying decisions. A brand with a favorable impression becomes a trusted asset and an extension of the customer's lifestyle or personality.

PRODUCT IS PERCEIVED AS HIGH QUALITY, THEN A HIGHER COST IS EXPECTED

6. A brand's pricing strategy is based on the consumers' perception of its value.

Many managers are unaware of how price should relate to what a customer thinks and expects from a product or service, and as a result they can make the mistake of charging too little or too much. The right balance of quality, cost, price and consumer expectations of the product and brand can be tough to achieve, but is well worth the effort and study to build customer satisfaction. If a product is perceived as high quality, then it's expected that a higher cost will follow. But if a company cuts corners on quality to increase profitability and consumers notice the difference, the brand could suffer long-term damage and take years to recoup its perception of quality.

7. The brand's product family and hierarchy make sense within the larger brand identity.

Many companies have multiple product brands under the main brand umbrella. For a strong brand, it's important that sub-brands make sense in the overall brand family identity.

8. The brand is properly positioned against its competitors.

When a brand is well positioned, it fills a particular niche in the consumer's mind. That's because these brands have worked hard over time to build and maintain their niche in the public's awareness by emphasizing their distinct differentiators from their competitors.

9. The company's managers and employees understand what the brand means to consumers.

With strong brands, the managers and employees appreciate and understand the personality of the brand and how consumers perceive it. When it's clear what customers like and don't like about the brand and what qualities they associate with the brand, then managers will know in advance if a specific action will make sense within the brand personality.

10. The company monitors various media sources to manage its brand equity.

Strong brands conduct regular checkups and brand-tracking studies to determine the health of the brand's identity. This may consist of a detailed review of how the elements of the brand have been used in all marketing and communications during the recent past. It may also be done externally through consumer focus groups, online data and surveys.

11. The brand is given adequate resource support and that support is sustained over the long run.

Brand equity is built carefully and intentionally over time by sustained brand awareness. Think of Harley Davidson motorcycles. Over the years this company, through community building and brand building efforts, has created a cult-like status.

(Original Source: The Brand Report Card by Kevin Lane Keller published in Harvard Business Review)

```
+01.93%  99.82  253
+01.56%  74.59  619
-00.27%  64 92  174
-06.95%  25 36  54
48  +00.13%  35.95  211
23  +08.69%  71.24  21
75  +06.93%  54.43  3
56  -01.73%  78  43
53  +02.59%  98.86
92  +08.49%  39.03
38 .92           88.7
         90%
```

WHAT DOES THAT MEAN TO YOU?

How do these attributes of strong brands help you? As stated at the beginning of this book, a familiar, recognizable brand has the ability to get noticed and remembered. When your brand is strong and aligned, it pays you in dividends—greater market share, higher customer awareness, and more repeat sales. When it's weak and out of alignment, it's like driving a car when the wheels are out of alignment—it might get you where you want to go and then again, it might not.

How much of your resources are dedicated to building your company's brand? Your brand is much like an investment. It needs to have a strategy, goals, regular check-ups and a maintenance program to stay strong and growing.

Think of your brand as a primary business asset.

When you look at your daily calendar, how much time do you invest in building your brand equity strategy each quarter? Each month? Or even each week?

☐ 5 hours ☐ 10 hours ☐ 20 hours ☐ 30 hours

YOUR ENTIRE COMPANY SHOULD BE YOUR BRANDING DEPARTMENT.

CUSTOMERS ARE INTERESTED IN "WHY YOU SELL" AS MUCH AS "WHAT YOU SELL." WHO YOUR COMPANY IS AND WHY IT IS IN BUSINESS WILL NEED TO BE CLEARLY DEFINED. SUCCESSFUL BRANDS WILL FOCUS ON LIVING THE BRAND AND MARKETING FROM THE INSIDE OUT. MARKETING CAN NO LONGER BE A DEPARTMENT. EVERYONE MUST BE ABLE TO COMMUNICATE THE COMPANY'S MISSION AND VISION, BECOMING, IN EFFECT, BRAND AMBASSADORS.

INVESTING IN BRAND EQUITY

Though a brand is an intangible "thing," marketing researchers believe that it is one of the most important things a business can own. The image, personality, name recognition, identity, reputation and positive attitudes associated with a company and its products are referred to as its brand equity. It is the extra value that influences a customer's decisions to purchase your product or service, even if a competitive product has similar features and a lower price.

There is disagreement among researchers about how to accurately measure a brand's equity, but Interbrand, the world's leading brand consultancy, has developed a brand valuation model that has become ISO certified (International Organization for Standardization).

WELL-LEVERAGED BRANDS PRODUCE HIGHER RETURNS TO SHAREHOLDERS

Interbrand's ranking and valuation of the world's top brands is based on a combination of attributes that they believe contribute to a brand's cumulative value:

- The financial performance of the branded products and services
- The role the brand plays in influencing customer choice
- The strength the brand has to command a premium price or secure earnings for the company

Regardless of the methods used, all researchers agree that strong, well-leveraged brands produce higher returns to shareholders than weaker, less well-known brands. This means that brand and brand awareness have the potential to positively impact shareholder value and future sales. Building brand equity is the responsibility of everyone involved with a company's profitability all the way up to the CEO.

THE BRAND EQUITY MODEL

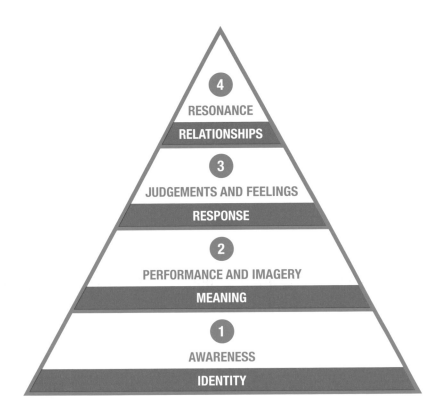

The premise of Keller's Brand Equity Model is that the power of a brand resides in the minds of its customers. It starts with ensuring a customer can identify the brand and associate the brand with a product/service establishing positive opinions that ultimately lead to converting brand responses to build loyal relationships between the customer and the brand.

STAND FOR SOMETHING. AND YOU'LL STAND OUT.

In an article in *Forbes Magazine*, it was suggested that the #2 reason 8 out of 10 businesses fail is due to no differentiation in the marketplace.

According to Dr. J. Walter Smith, the head of Yankelovich Research, "Advertising clutter is the single biggest problem with marketing. Not just today, but as long as advertising has been around. People are annoyed by ads that show up in unfamiliar places, but become used to them over time. So marketers respond by finding even more unfamiliar places. It's cumulative and it's getting worse. Yet, consumers can process no more information today than they could before, and perhaps even less."

8 OUT OF 10 BUSINESSES FAIL DUE TO NO DIFFERENTIATION IN THE MARKET

In this environment, standing out from your competition and being noticed and remembered by your prospect and customer is not only crucial for your business to compete; it's a matter of success or failure.

After years of working with various companies and brands, we learned that the most effective strategy in standing out is to first identify who you are (your authentic self) and why you do what you do (your purpose) and then integrate these into every part of your business.

If you were asked the question, "Why are you in business?" your first thought may be, "Well, we're in business to make a profit and to grow, of course." All businesses need to grow—and profit makes the wheels of commerce turn and enables good businesses to grow and do great things.

But in today's over-congested business landscape, offering a product or service with competitive features isn't enough to stand out. Just do a quick search for your product or service online and you'll see how many competing companies offer very similar products or services to yours.

WHERE DOES YOUR BRAND STAND AMONG COMPETITORS?

One of the steps in standing out is to have a clear picture of where you're standing now compared to everyone else. Like a GPS directional device, our Brand Positioning Assessment shows you where you are compared to the competition and competing brands.

It measures four key attributes of your brand:

Brand Differentiation – How effectively does your brand capture the attention of prospects?

Brand Relevance – How aligned is your brand to your customers' and prospects' needs?
The results of these two brand attributes determine your overall **Brand Distinction**.

Brand Promise – How consistently does your brand deliver on its promises?

Brand Intelligence – How well does your company understand its brand and the quality and impact of the brand experience on your customers?
The results of these two attributes determine your **Brand Equity**.

A well-known and respected brand adds additional value (equity) to a company's products and services and will positively influence a customer's buying decision even when faced with a competitive product with similar features and a comparable price. Many market researchers agree that brand equity is one of the most important assets a company can own. It also adds value when selling a business.

BRAND POSITIONING ASSESSMENT

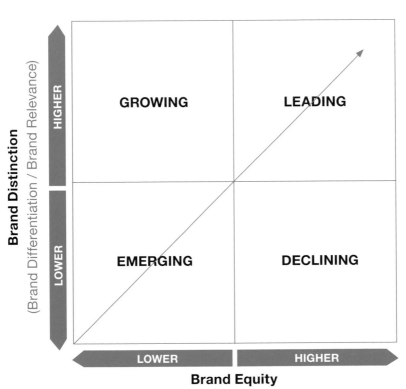

Brand Distinction
(Brand Differentiation / Brand Relevance)

HIGHER

LOWER

GROWING

LEADING

EMERGING

DECLINING

LOWER

HIGHER

Brand Equity
(Brand Promise / Brand Intelligence)

Brand Positioning Assessment: Rate your Brand Distinction and Brand Equity on a scale of 1-10 (5 being the mid level between lower and higher); then, do the same for your competitors to assess where your brand stands in comparison to competing companies.

NOW THAT WE'RE CLEAR ON WHAT "BRAND" IS,
LET'S LOOK AT MASTERING THE EIGHT FUNDAMENTALS
TO STAND OUT FROM THE COMPETITION.

THE ORGANIZATION KNOWS AND LIVES ITS PURPOSE; IT KNOWS WHAT IT STANDS FOR AND IS TRUE TO ITS BELIEFS.

PURPOSE

IDENTIFY WHERE YOU STAND.

Which of these statements most accurately reflects the current level of purpose in your company?

- ☐ Our purpose is not clear.
- ☐ Our purpose is somewhat clear.
- ☐ Our purpose is clear but we do not know what the organization stands for.
- ☐ Our purpose is clear and we know what we stand for but it is not consistently communicated.
- ☐ Our purpose is clear, we know what we stand for, everyone knows and understands it and it is consistently communicated.

WHEN YOU BEGAN YOUR BUSINESS, YOU HAD A PICTURE OF WHAT YOU WANTED TO ACCOMPLISH—A PLAN OR PURPOSE THAT YOU HOPED TO ACHIEVE THROUGH YOUR WORK. AND THERE WAS SOMETHING IN THAT PICTURE THAT WENT BEYOND THE IDEA OF MAKING MONEY. YOU WANTED TO "MAKE A DIFFERENCE."

But as your company has grown, it's possible that the picture you envisioned of your destination has become less clear, overshadowed by the day-to-day details of business. You're working hard. Your employees are working hard. You know the potential is there to do more, to climb higher, to work smarter, but you're just not sure how.

You recognize all the telltale signs that you're stalled—sales are less than projected or sluggish; managers and departments seem to be struggling to get on the same page; response or turn around times are slow; and on some level things just feel out of sync.

When your company is in a slump, has reached a plateau, gotten stalled, lost its edge or whatever description you use, it's likely that you're out of touch with your purpose. This is the inspirational driving force, the energy and enthusiasm that first got your business rolling. And it's an essential fundamental to keep your business rolling and growing.

Your purpose is not a mission or vision statement. Mission statements describe the type of business you're in and possibly define your audience. Vision statements are about where your company wants to be in the future.

Purpose includes the core values and beliefs that are the unchanging principles, ideas and philosophies that guide your decisions. They serve to create a particular culture and environment within a company and include things like belief in diversity, fair and equal treatment of employees, a commitment to honesty and integrity, ensuring a safe and supportive work environment, contributing to your local community and the like.

Your "Why" is another term used to describe the compelling reason behind your actions. A company's "Why" is a demonstration of who it is and what it stands for—its values and beliefs put into action.

Purpose integrates what a company values and believes in with why it's in business and describes them in terms of the heart as well as the mind. Purpose is the beneficial something more that a company delivers that adds significant value to whatever it sells.

"THE TWO MOST IMPORTANT DAYS IN YOUR LIFE ARE THE DAY YOU WERE BORN AND THE DAY YOU FOUND OUT WHY."
– MARK TWAIN

BENEFITS OF WORKING FROM YOUR PURPOSE

Doing business with a clear purpose makes everything work better and ultimately serves to make yours a better company. Your brand's purpose should be implemented into your organization and explained to every member of your team. Living and working from your purpose daily can be transformative for your company.

PURPOSE ADDS SIGNIFICANT VALUE TO WHATEVER A COMPANY SELLS

The value that a company creates should be measured not just in terms of short-term profits or paychecks but also in terms of how it sustains the conditions that allow it to flourish over time. Companies with purpose deliver more than just financial returns; they also build enduring institutions.

This social or institutional logic lies behind the practices of many widely admired, high-performing, and enduring companies. In those firms, society and people are not afterthoughts or inputs to be used and discarded, but are core to the purpose of their business.

Here are a few reasons why:

Get noticed and remembered—People will notice your company and your products or services because you're not just selling another commodity, you're selling a product that will make a difference in the quality of your customers' lives.

Connects you to others—Customers feel more connected to businesses that stand for something beyond a sale; people learn to trust a company that is interested in the quality of their lives and proves it through action.

Builds relationships—Knowing and sharing your purpose helps people relate to you emotionally. In any relationship, sharing who you are encourages understanding and compassion.

Makes lasting impressions—Sharing your purpose creates rich ground for a relationship to take root, grow and flourish. Customers may forget a product and who sells it, but they don't forget a relationship.

Provides focus—Knowing your organization's purpose and implementing it throughout your business allows you and your team to focus on what really matters to grow the business.

Energizes your operations—Your goals and mission become clearer, engaging and energizing for your entire team when there's an expressed purpose behind what they do. It supports better company morale and employee retention and it attracts the kind of customers who will share your product or service with others.

Fuels growth—Purpose empowers your business decisions, shapes marketing campaigns and supports clearer and meaningful communications. It guides you in hiring the right people that fit with your values and beliefs.

"EFFORTS AND COURAGE ARE NOT ENOUGH WITHOUT PURPOSE AND DIRECTION."
– JOHN F. KENNEDY

DISCOVERING YOUR PURPOSE

Are you unsure about your business's purpose? Possibly you never thought about it in these terms before but have a general concept of what purpose means. Answer the questions below and you can gain a clearer idea of what your purpose is and how it fits into what your business does.

What do you love? What activities do you most enjoy?

What does the world need? What do you do that adds value to the world?

What do you do really well? What are your talents and skills?

What would the world pay for it? What do you do that others value and want, and how much do they want it?

Now look at the illustration on the next page to see how your purpose connects with and supports the driving force behind your business.

. . . .

"SUCCESS DEMANDS SINGLENESS OF PURPOSE."
– VINCE LOMBARDI

. . . .

WHAT IS YOUR PURPOSE?

....

Purpose Exercise: Engage your team to discuss each of the aspects that lead to discovering an organization's purpose. Break into small groups and share outcomes.

....

WHAT IS YOUR PURPOSE?

WHAT YOU LOVE:

WHAT THE WORLD NEEDS:

WHAT YOU DO REALLY WELL:

WHAT THE WORLD WILL PAY FOR IT:

Purpose Worksheet: Use this worksheet to record exercise outcomes: What do you love? What does the world need? What do you do really well? What is the world willing to pay for it?

WHAT DO YOU STAND FOR?

Now more than ever, your company's success is determined by how clearly you define and communicate your core values and qualities. In short, it's all about what you stand for. What do you stand for? Whether your business is established or new, you have to know what you stand for before your customers can know. Do you know? What is it that makes you stand out? What separates you from the competition? You may be thinking that you have excellent customer service, a quality product or solid reputation. Guess what? So does everyone else. You need to think more deeply and thoroughly about what makes your business distinctive and unique.

Why does it matter? While it may be worthy to note that you have a quality product and great service, these qualities, in themselves, are not enough to distinguish you from the crowd. In today's overcrowded marketplace, your success is determined by your clarity about what you stand for and how you communicate that purpose to the world. Knowing what you and your company stand for is the competitive advantage in any industry. It's how you stand out. So, step out of the crowd. Stand for something.

Knowing what you stand for makes everything perform efficiently with purpose, including hiring, business decisions, marketing campaigns and internal communications. It guides you in hiring the right people that have the same values and purpose. It leads to better company morale and less turnover.

Look closely at some truly great companies, outstanding companies, and memorable companies. You'll see that they offer good products—sometimes, great products—though most of all they stand out because they make a difference in people's lives. And they make defining their purpose an integral part of who they are and what they do.

Author Jim Collins in his book *Good To Great* says: "What you stand for should be the basis for every decision and the touchstone for all your actions. What you stand for should be clear to every employee, vendor and colleague in your business. And it should be consistent across every channel of communication. What you stand for shapes the impact you have on the world and makes the difference between building a company that is ordinary or extraordinary."

WHAT YOU STAND FOR SHAPES THE IMPACT YOU HAVE ON THE WORLD

Identifying the characteristics that distinguish a company from its competitors has never been more essential for success than it is now. Online reach and global media have drawn every industry in to international focus. With these changes come expanded opportunities, but also expanded exposure. If a company does not tell its own story, someone else may very well tell one about them.

The question has become not only how can you stand out, but what will you stand for? It's crucial that you direct how your business distinguishes itself in the marketplace.

Standing out is a function of several things—understanding and promoting the purpose behind your business and what guides you to do what you do; identifying your authentic self—your company's personality and personal stories and then integrating these into your marketing and communications efforts; and finally managing and promoting your reputation within the landscape of different communication media.

All organizations must stand out to be successful, but some companies manage to stand out continuously for many years. It's not that they don't have competition, but they repeatedly support innovation and a dedication to excellence. They are truly at the top of their class.

Here are a few examples:

Apple Inc.—Since its founding in 1976, Apple has been on the cutting edge of technology at a time when the fledgling industry was wide open. While the Apple technology was not necessarily better than the others, from the beginning, it has always come from a fresh perspective which continues through today. This perspective has taken the technology of the computer and varied its form (ipad, ipod, iphone, iwatch, icar) and its application (music, telephone, visuals) so that the brand has been rated as the most valuable in the world on Forbes list of 100 Most Valuable Brands for five consecutive years.

Panera Bread—Panera is personally invested in the state of the nation's health. The company wants to serve food that they would eat themselves and prepare for their own children. They care about how their food is made, sourced, handled and prepared. They voluntarily post calories on their menus, remove artificial ingredients and offer poultry raised without antibiotics. They have changed the status quo for fast food restaurants, proactively setting a higher standard for themselves and their industry.

Disney (The Walt Disney Company)—From its early beginnings as a small cartoon studio in 1923, Disney has expanded its organization to include parks and resorts, consumer products, interactive, movie studio entertainment and media while keeping true to its goal of providing quality entertainment experiences for the entire family. For many the name Disney is synonymous with the word "magic."

Life Is Good—Inspired by the desire to counter the daily flood of negative news by spreading the power of optimism, in 1994 two brothers, already in the t-shirt trade, created the Life Is Good series with the now well-known illustration of "Jake." The idea and the business took off. Today, Life is Good continues to spread its own brand of optimism online, in airports and community shops and donates 10 percent of its net profits to help kids in need.

Warby Parker—Warby Parker is a company that believes that every idea starts with a problem. Theirs was simple: glasses are too expensive. When they realized that the eyewear industry is dominated by a single company who has been able to keep prices artificially high, they decided to create an alternative. Their lofty objective is to offer designer eyewear at a revolutionary price and lead the way for socially conscious businesses.

WeWork—WeWork transforms buildings into collaborative workspaces where shared workspace, community, and services are provided for entrepreneurs, freelancers, startups and small businesses. Their mission is to create a world where people work to make a life, not just a living.

Kickstarter—Kickstarter is the world's largest funding platform for creative projects. It was built to help bring creative projects to life. In 2015, Kickstarter became a Benefit Corporation. These are for-profit companies that are obligated to consider the impact of their decisions on society, not only shareholders. Radically, positive impact on society becomes part of a Benefit Corporation's legally defined goals.

Etsy—Etsy is a peer-to-peer e-commerce website focused on handmade or vintage items and supplies, as well as unique factory-manufactured items. Their mission is to reimagine commerce in ways that build a more fulfilling and lasting world.

IKEA—IKEA is a multinational group of companies that designs and sells ready-to-assemble furniture, appliances, small motor vehicles and home accessories. The IKEA concept is to furnish the world, one home at a time. The concept comes from a place of values that emerge from the heart. Its culture is one of enthusiasm, togetherness, willpower and hard work born from its Swedish roots.

WHY WE LOVE SOUTHWEST

We fly a lot. And we couldn't do it without Southwest Airlines. We were sitting in a terminal at the airport and looked out the window and saw a baggage carrier go by bearing a sign that said "Wave at your luggage." Then the man driving waved at us. Southwest lives their purpose.They let you bring your bags for free. And they give us the freedom to fly. That is what Southwest stands for: The Freedom to Fly. We know Southwest loves us. They remember our birthday and send us drink coupons. They are friendly. They make our lives easier.

Author Roy Spence wrote about Southwest Airlines in his book, *It's Not What You Sell, It's What You Stand For*. He tells the story of two guys who wanted to make flights between Texas cities cheaper and more available. Herb Kelleher and Rollin King started with that purpose and then created an airline that allowed people the opportunity to fly, once a service available to only 15 percent of the American public. Southwest knows what they stand for and they live it.

. . . .

"A COMPANY IS STRONGER IF IT IS BOUND BY LOVE RATHER THAN BY FEAR."
– HERB KELLEHER, SOUTHWEST AIRLINES

. . . .

BIG SKY IDEAS:
DIAMONDS ARE A BRAND'S BEST FRIEND

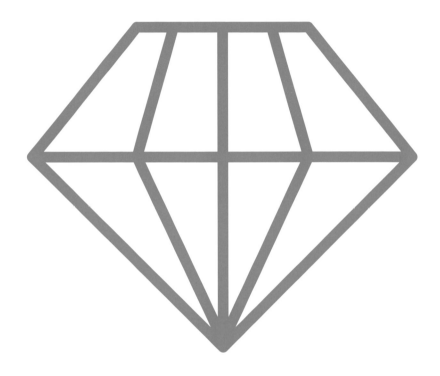

Diamond Mining Exercise: Look for opportunities to improve your products and services. Poll your team and ask these questions: Where are the diamonds in our own back yard? What is the next idea that is going to take us to the next level? What big sky idea is going to help us stand out?

WHAT YOU WOULD DO IF...

MONEY WAS NOT AN ISSUE:

YOU COULD PURSUE YOUR FAVORITE THING TO DO:

YOU COULD EXPLORE YOUR INTERESTS:

YOU COULD START OVER:

Purpose What If Exercise: What if? What would you do if money was not an issue? The goal is to discover what you and your team are passionate about and look for ways to bring that passion into discovering your purpose.

REPUTATION HAS BECOME THE BIG CHALLENGE
IN TODAY'S ONLINE ENVIRONMENT. IT'S HARD TO KNOW
WHAT'S TRUE AND WHAT ISN'T.

THE ORGANIZATION MONITORS BRAND PERCEPTION, INDUSTRY TRENDS AND THE COMPETITIVE LANDSCAPE.

REPUTATION

IDENTIFY WHERE YOU STAND.

Which of these statements most accurately reflects the current level of reputation monitoring and online awareness that exists in your company?

- [ ] Our reputation is not clear.
- [ ] Our reputation is somewhat clear.
- [ ] Our reputation is clear but we do not monitor it online; nor do we monitor our competition.
- [ ] Our reputation is clear, our online awareness is monitored but we do not monitor our competitors.
- [ ] Our reputation is clear, our online awareness is monitored monthly and we consistently monitor our competitors.

YOUR REPUTATION IS YOUR CURRENCY. COMPANIES WITH STRONG POSITIVE REPUTATIONS ATTRACT BETTER TALENT AND ARE PERCEIVED AS DELIVERING MORE VALUE THROUGH THEIR PRODUCTS AND SERVICES. THEIR CUSTOMERS ARE MORE LOYAL AND BUY BROADER RANGES OF PRODUCTS AND SERVICES. THIS MAKES ORGANIZATIONS ESPECIALLY VULNERABLE TO ANYTHING THAT DAMAGES THEIR REPUTATIONS.

THE POWER OF KNOWING

When we were little, our dad used to say "You don't know what you don't know." It was constant. He would drop us off at school, roll down the window and holler "Winnie and Lorrie—you don't know what you don't know." We would bow our heads quietly and keep going. Birthdays, friends over, Sunday dinners, he would say, "You don't know what you don't know." We would look at him and say "yeah dad…"

It took us a long time to "get it"—to understand what he was trying to teach us—to understand why he kept repeating himself and how it became a core way of thinking in our upbringing.

Fast forward to today—there is so much out there that we don't know. Do you know the condition of your business's reputation? Do you know what people are saying about your business and brand? If not, then you need to get a clearer picture of these external perceptions because not knowing what your customers and prospects are saying can be toxic to your growth.

Once upon a time, companies did not have to worry much about what customers had to say about their brands. Customers' opinions were shared with only the few people they knew and wanted to tell. Today, communication is a wide-open book where customers can share their thoughts, opinions, compliments, complaints, about companies anytime and anywhere.

Today, a customer's negative opinion about your company or its products can be spread around the world within moments and remain there available for others to read for years. So how do you protect your reputation in this kind of world?

EONE IS TALKING ABOUT YOUR BRAND RIGHT NOW. WHAT ARE THEY SAYING?

Here are a few steps we recommend:

Monitor religiously—Track what is being said about your company, both the positive and negative comments, across all media as if your reputation depends on it. Because it does. Make consistent monitoring of your reputation your mantra—because negative perceptions and comments can, overnight, wreck a reputation that you've built through years of hard work. And by monitoring, you can better plan your responses.

Communicate, communicate, communicate—Honest and sincere communication is key to any healthy relationship and communicating with customers and would-be customers is no different.

Respond—Stay aware of your customers' perceptions and comments so you can respond to both positive and negative feedback in a timely manner. A slow response communicates indecisiveness or worse, apathy. A timely response can help your company avoid or limit possible damage to your reputation.

Build goodwill—By being proactive and building goodwill through ongoing positive actions, a company can stay "ahead of the curve" and build a positive reputation that can lead to increased customer loyalty and minimize the damage of negative criticism.

BUSINESS IS BUILT ON TRUST

We've often said that business is built on relationships. And the basis of all business relationships is trust—internally within your employee team and externally with prospects, customers and vendors. It's not only the foundation of strong relationships, but a source of distinct advantage and an essential strategy for your survival and success. In fact, Forbes magazine states that trust is "the most valuable commodity in today's business world."

"WHICH WOULD YOU RATHER? TALK TO CUSTOMERS NOW OR TALK TO CUSTOMERS THOUSANDS OF DOLLARS DOWN THE ROAD AND STILL FIND OUT YOU WERE WRONG."
— NAIL IT, THEN SCALE IT.

ASK YOUR CUSTOMERS

One of the best ways to understand how your company is perceived externally, is to talk with your customers—not just to communicate to your customers, but communicate with them.

In a two-way dialogue, you listen to what your customers have to say about their experience doing business with your company and you explain to them what you're doing to fill their needs and make their lives easier.

In an article for *Forbes Magazine*, entrepreneur Eric T. Wagner says that the top three reasons that eight out of ten businesses fail are:

1) They're not really in touch with their customers through deep dialogue.
2) They have no real differentiation in the market.
3) They don't clearly communicate their true value proposition.

Deep dialogue, he explains, is imperative for a business—it means having regular conversations with customers to understand their point of view—their pains, behaviors, dreams and values. And what better way to understand what your customers want than by asking them.

Speak to customers as if you were sitting with them, in person, instead of composing a press release or reading a questionnaire. Be genuine when talking and express your interest in their opinion.

Then listen… listen openly to what they have to say instead of missing their words while mentally preparing a response. Giving your full attention to a customer will make a lasting impression and give you new insights into what your customers truly think and feel about your business. And always take what your customer tells you seriously. Let them know how valuable their opinion is by finding ways to act on their feedback and make improvements in your product, service, delivery system, or other area of your operations of which you were unaware. And your ability to serve them better in the future will be enhanced.

Say thank you. Show your customers you appreciate their time and their opinion by offering your thanks at the end of your conversation. Show gratitude for each person who uses your product or service; express kindness and compassion for their opinion and their business and you'll attract more of the same.

If you're a business owner or senior manager, don't rely on your customer service department to do all the talking; pick up the phone and have a conversation with a customer yourself. It will help you stay in touch with the reality of your company and what keeps it in business.

Follow up and follow through. In your conversations with customers, if you say you'll look into something that you talk about, find an answer to a question the customer asks, or that you'll do something about what caused them to have a negative experience, do it. Your word is your contract.

Following through on what you've said and then letting your customer know what was done will build trust, promote transparency and help cement your relationship. Manage the customer's expectations to ensure that you're not over promising, but always follow through and communicate the results of your conversation. It will grow customer relationships and turn your conversations into opportunities for improvement.

"YOUR BRAND IS THE SINGLE MOST IMPORTANT INVESTMENT YOU CAN MAKE IN YOUR BUSINESS."– STEVE FORBES

ARE YOU ACTIVELY MANAGING YOUR BRAND REPUTATION?

A large part of a company's market value comes from hard-to-assess intangible assets like brand equity and intellectual capital. This makes an organization especially vulnerable to anything that damages its reputation.

Communication in marketing has changed dramatically in recent years. According to marketingtechblog.com, 70 percent of business-to-consumer marketers have acquired customers through Facebook. 52 percent of online adults use two or more social media sites (Pew Research Center).

Communication is now a two-way process. Customers can research, interact with, and comment about companies for any reason to a worldwide audience of other potential customers. In this light, it's crucial that companies continuously monitor what is being said about their brands because there are endless forms of communication available between consumers.

REPUTATION. WHETHER IT REFLECTS WHO WE ARE OR NOT, WE ALL HAVE ONE.

Without knowledge about what is being said or written about your company and brand, you could be losing customers based on word-of-mouth interactions or customer reviews. Research has shown that many people trust these forms of communication more than traditional information sources, such as your website, printed material and advertisements. If you are not monitoring every channel of communication, your brand's reputation could be at risk before you even realize it.

> ## "IT TAKES 20 YEARS TO BUILD A REPUTATION AND FIVE MINUTES TO RUIN IT. IF YOU THINK ABOUT THAT, YOU'LL DO THINGS DIFFERENTLY." – WARREN BUFFET

Here are some examples of crisis situations that threatened some well-known brands:

Nike—Not long ago, Nike was criticized for low-wage foreign labor practices. It tarnished their image and hurt sales. But Nike turned their image around. By not denying every allegation and quickly changing their methods, Nike was able to remain a top athletic clothing brand.

British Petroleum was another brand whose image was damaged due to the 2010 oil spill in the Gulf of Mexico. Social media and viral videos spread the situation rapidly, making it an international issue within hours rather than days. BP responded quickly on their website with an apology and began immediately taking measures to fix the incident and prevent any further incidents from occurring, and they have continued reputation repair in the years since, across every channel and opportunity, including financial reparation and community service.

Unlike BP, **United Airlines** did not make an immediate formal response to a global computer system outage. This caused its already poor reputation to plummet further. The company's lack of communication caused frustrations to customers that will be remembered long after the problem was repaired and normalcy returned.

Reputation—whether it truly reflects who we are or not, we all have one. People compare themselves to others – it's part of human nature. They do the same with brands. Continuous awareness of external perceptions can be a critical factor to your success.

RISKS OF A DAMAGED REPUTATION

Building a reputation from scratch can be easy—no one knows who you are. You can build your brand up to be anything you want it to be. But a damaged reputation is much harder to rebuild. Customers are more likely to remember and discuss bad experiences over good experiences.

In a survey done by American Express in 2014, 60 percent of people said they always share their bad experiences and tell nearly three times more people about a bad experience than they do about a good one.

If your reputation is damaged, there are steps you can take to begin rebuilding if it's not beyond repair:

Take Responsibility: The first step is admitting that something is wrong. If a customer writes about a bad experience with your company, apologize to that customer on the same review. By doing this, the customer—and other consumers—will see that you are serious about fixing your mistakes. This alone could start to reshape the customer's opinion about your company.

Don't Ignore the Negative: Learn from customers' negative reviews. After all, reputation is based on what customers perceive to be true about your company. Understanding the source of negative perceptions can assist you in repairing possible weaknesses within your systems and processes.

Continuous Monitoring: In order to maintain a positive reputation, you must monitor your online footprint frequently. This can help your company become proactive in sustaining your brand's reputation.

Although bad reviews and press can seem terrible at the moment, a bad reputation can be turned around with conscientious effort and sincere concern.

These are a few tools that are especially useful in monitoring online conversations to give insights into what is being said and where. Some have features that allow you to track over time and respond to comments and questions within the platform in addition to monitoring:

☐ Google Alerts

☐ Social Mention

☐ Trackur

☐ Meltwater

☐ Radian6

A more extensive list of resources can be found at the back of this book.

A GOOD REPUTATION IS HARD TO BEAT.
A BAD REPUTATION IS HARD TO OVERCOME.

REPUTATION SENTIMENT

Social media channels have created a new world for the expression of customer opinion. It is immediate and immortal. **Do you know the quality of your brand's online sentiment and engagement?**

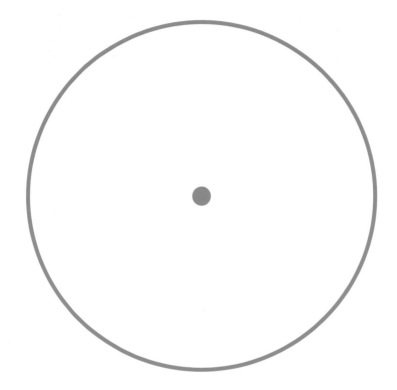

Reputation Sentiment Exercise: Review your last 30 days of online mentions using a listening tool and separate by sentiment—positive, negative and neutral. Divide the pie into sections. (Ex. 3/4 positive, 1/4 negative and 1/4 neutral.) Set a goal to increase positive sentiment with specific actions.

WHAT VALUE DO YOU DELIVER?

WHAT IS YOUR PRIMARY VALUE PROPOSITION?

WHAT ARE YOUR SECONDARY VALUE PROPOSITIONS?

Value Proposition Exercise: Poll your employee team. Ask what they believe is the company's primary value proposition. Collect the feedback and choose the value proposition most often mentioned as your number one. List the next five most frequent mentions as your secondary value propositions.

RUMOR SAYS

WHAT I'VE HEARD:

WHAT IS TRUE:

Reputation Rumor Exercise: Brainstorm on key topics relative to your company, brand, products, customers and competitors. Look for ways to neutralize rumors and leverage truths.

WE MAKE DECISIONS ABOUT WHAT WE THINK ABOUT BRANDS IN A MATTER OF SECONDS, WITHOUT KNOWING VERY MUCH ABOUT WHAT LIES BELOW THE SURFACE.

THE OUTWARD APPEARANCE OF THE BRAND TRULY REFLECTS WHO THE ORGANIZATION IS AND THE VALUE IT DELIVERS.

VISUALITY

IDENTIFY WHERE YOU STAND.

Which of these statements most accurately reflects the current level of how the outward appearance of the brand reflects who the company is and the value it delivers:

- ☐ The outward appearance of our brand does not reflect who we are or the value we deliver.
- ☐ The outward appearance of our brand somewhat reflects who we are and the value we deliver.
- ☐ The outward appearance of our brand is unique, reflects who we are and the value we deliver, but looks similar to competing brands.
- ☐ The outward appearance of our brand is unique, reflects who we are and the value we deliver, but could use an upgrade.
- ☐ The outward appearance of our brand is a true reflection of who we are and reflects the value we deliver.

FIRST IMPRESSIONS. GROWING UP AS A TWIN, YOU GET USED TO THE SURPRISED DOUBLE TAKE LOOK YOU GET WHEN SOMEONE REALIZES FOR THE FIRST TIME THAT YOU'RE HALF OF A SET OF TWINS. FIRST IMPRESSIONS STICK WITH PEOPLE. EVERYONE IN BUSINESS IS AWARE OF THE POWER OF FIRST IMPRESSIONS. THAT'S WHY THE WAY YOUR BRAND LOOKS IS A CRUCIAL ASPECT OF PRESENTING THE MOST ACCURATE VISUAL REPRESENTATION OF YOUR DISTINCT ADVANTAGE. **"VISUALITY" WE CALL IT. IT'S ONE OF THE MOST IMPORTANT FUNDAMENTALS— ONE THAT WE'VE BEEN STUDYING OUR ENTIRE LIVES.**

How can you present your business through design in a way that honestly describes your business and is a visual first impression of how you wish to be known by others?

People trained in brand strategy like ourselves love to talk about the visual side of branding because it's the fundamental that's closest to our hearts. However, good branding blends strategic and creative perspectives. Like yin and yang, balance is what differentiates good design. Good design makes a powerful first impression and ensures your company is noticed and remembered. No small thing, visuality.

TALK THE TALK. WALK THE WALK. LOOK THE PART.

Words, actions and visuals are the tools that are used to demonstrate the authenticity of the purpose of your company. Consider "trading places" with your customers or competition. The experience gives you the chance to learn and find new insights. It allows you to view your business from a different pair of eyes so that you can gain new perspective.

A lot of people ask my identical twin and I if we've ever traded places. The answer is yes. In junior high school, we decided that the best time for us to try switching places was on Halloween. It was the first time that we thought we would actually be able to get away with it. We went to school that day in costumes handmade by our grandmother, dressed as Raggedy Ann dolls. We thought it would take the matching costumes and makeup to be able to switch places. Sure enough, we exchanged classes that day and no one ever knew the difference.

We realize now that we didn't need the costumes and makeup to actually pull it off, but that was the only time we intentionally traded places. However, we're still trading places today without actually doing anything. People often just assume we're the other twin!

In these situations, we don't say anything. We learn. It gives us great perspective about the life and relationships of the other twin; we get the chance to learn more and gain insight.

This has also taught us how to "trade places" with others in our lives. While we can't do it as easily as we can swap identities with each other, we take the time to imagine what it might be like to be our clients or our competitors.

Here is a simple exercise that all businesses should regularly attempt. An easy way to do this is to look at your own online presence. In fact your whole team can do this exercise and learn something. Pretend that you are one of your own customers and search for your business online. What comes up? What doesn't come up?

What does your website look like to someone who knows nothing about your business? What does your LinkedIn or Facebook page look like? Would you respond to your own tweets and read the links that you post? Are you interested in your own blog's content? Compare your pages to others and see the differences that consumers or competitors might notice right away. Try to view everything objectively.

Now imagine that you are one of your competitors. Look at your website and social networks from their point of view. Be as neutral as possible. Do you see any flaws or weaknesses? What are your competitors doing better?

WHEN YOU ARE ABLE TO SEE YOURSELF OUTSIDE OF YOURSELF, YOU SEE THE WORLD THROUGH AN ENTIRELY DIFFERENT LENS.

PEOPLE DO JUDGE A BOOK BY IT'S COVER

The saying "don't judge a book by its cover" is a metaphorical phrase which means "you shouldn't prejudge the worth or value of something by its outward appearance alone." But guess what? We do.

As twins, we've developed a heightened awareness of the importance of perception and reality. Being constantly mistaken for my sister and vice versa can do that.

Lorrie and I share the distinct advantage of having a living mirror reflection of what we look like from outside ourselves. Now, like no one else, she can view me from the outside and honestly say, "We look terrible in that shade of yellow." Or, "I'm not sure if you realize that when you said such and such, it actually came across like something else." Or, "Yes, that design may be out-of-the-box-creative, but is it consistent with the client's brand, and how can we measure its success?"

From the first-hand experience of dealing with misperceptions and working hard to refine our individual identities, we've honed the ability to perceive distinct differences in other people, other companies and other brands. And in our line of work, we're able to use this ability to help our client/brands learn to see themselves more objectively.

. . . .

EVEN THOUGH FIRST IMPRESSIONS ARE IMPORTANT, THEY'RE ALSO OFTEN BASED ON VERY LIMITED INFORMATION THAT MAY INCLUDE MOODS, PRIOR MEMORIES OR EXPERIENCES.

. . . .

SYMBOLS HAVE MEANING.
WHICH OF THESE SYMBOLS WOULD YOU ASSOCIATE WITH YOUR BRAND?

IT'S ALL ABOUT THEM

Very likely the first impression a potential customer may have of your company will be a visual combination of words and images—a billboard, television commercial, advertisement or the result of an online search.

Companies are often inclined to be inner-focused in their communications. After all, their products and services are what they are most familiar with and most proud of. When they describe their products and services, their language may tend to "we" statements like "We can do this;" or "Our product can do that." Truth is, your prospects and customers are far more interested in what your product or service does for them. Will it save them time or money? Will it make them happier or healthier? These are the things that will motivate them to buy.

For your marketing efforts to be effective, you must learn to view your company from your customers' perspectives—to see yourself from outside yourself. Replace the "we" in your communications with you. "You will save 30 minutes each day that you use this product; or "Your house will be a more enjoyable place to live with this service." With every customer communication, ask yourself: How will this benefit the customer? How will this affect their experience of our brand? Will the customers see this as valuable and will it fill their needs?

· ·

"THE MOST POWERFUL BRANDS ARE BUILT FROM THE HEART. THEIR FOUNDATIONS ARE STRONGER BECAUSE THEY ARE BUILT WITH THE STRENGTH OF THE HUMAN SPIRIT, NOT AN AD CAMPAIGN."—HOWARD SCHULTZ, STARBUCKS"

· ·

FACE VALUE

Professor of psychology at Princeton University, Alexander Todorov, was fascinated by the social psychology of faces during his years as an undergraduate student. He noted that research had shown how even the glimpse of a face could create a strong impression on an observer based on as little as specific facial features. Previous research studies had found that thin lips and wrinkles at the corners of someone's eyes communicated that a person was intelligent, distinguished or determined. Persons with baby-faces were judged as being naïve and physically weak yet also honest and kind. Attractiveness was often equated with competence and masculinity with dominance. Not surprisingly, people also frequently said that they liked faces with features similar to their own.

Todorov conducted a major study at Princeton on the outcome of elections to learn if simple images of candidates that prompted "quick, unreflective judgments based solely on their facial appearances," would influence voting more than what a candidate believes or says, despite millions of dollars spent on their political information campaigns.

Those people surveyed rated photographic images of previous congressional candidates for traits of competence. The results showed that "candidates perceived as more competent turned out to have won 71.6% of the Senate races and 66.8% of the House races—far more than chance alone might allow. This single trait of competence projected by the candidate's photographic image influenced the outcome of political races more than all other traits combined."

DOPPELGANGERS

A doppelganger is defined as a look-alike or double of a living person, sometimes portrayed as a paranormal phenomenon, and in some traditions as a harbinger of bad luck (the evil twin).

In advertising, doppelganger has a couple of different meanings. One form of the phenomenon is ads or logos that are intentionally created to look like a familiar brand, altered by digital technology. A more insidious influence is the creation of an actual campaign to undermine the competition. In 2006, Apple created the "I'm a Mac" campaign that contrasted the speed of the Mac and PC computers in a humorous fashion. Not only did the campaign go viral, but it also helped grow sales for Apple by an estimated 39%.

Markus Geisler gives this definition in the AMA Journal of Marketing: "A doppelganger brand image is a family of disparaging images and stories about a brand that are circulated in popular culture by a loosely organized network of consumers, anti-brand activists, bloggers, and opinion leaders in the news and entertainment media." Underscore "disparaging" as these are generally negative: You should consider "Starsucks" for "Starbucks." Not only well-known brands are affected and not all campaigns take the form of harmless puns.

While many of these disparaging inferences may have no basis in fact, the most dangerous ones do. Consider using this information as a diagnostic tool to proactively manage the vulnerabilities of your emotional branding efforts.

FEELING BLUE?

Much discussion has been given to the psychology of color in marketing. While many believe that color is too personal a matter to be universally applicable to trends, there are some research-backed insights that have merit and warrant consideration here.

In the study *Impact of Color in Marketing*, it was determined that people make up their minds within 90 seconds of their initial interaction with a product and that 62 – 90% of the assessment is based on color alone. Prudent use of color can contribute not only to differentiation but to attitudes towards products.

In the course of her studies into the Dimensions of Brand Personality, psychologist and Stanford professor, Jennifer Aaker, has concluded that there is a real connection between the use of colors and customers' perceptions of a brand's personality. Her findings indicate that certain colors broadly align with specific traits, i.e., brown with ruggedness, purple with sophistication, and red with excitement. In addition, and in agreement with other academic research, such as *The Interactive Effects of Color*, she suggests that the importance is that the brand's colors support the personality being portrayed rather than align with stereotypical color associations. In other words, color has to "fit."

The bottom line is that there are no easy, clear-cut guidelines for choosing a brand's colors, but color is an absolutely essential consideration. Color is the feeling, mood, and image that your brand creates, and these play a subtle role in persuasion.

And for new brands, try to specifically target logo colors that ensure differentiation from entrenched competitors.

TWO-TENTHS OF A SECOND

According to researchers at the Missouri University of Science and Technology, it takes less than two-tenths of a second for an online visitor to form a first opinion of your brand once they've perused your company's website. Following that, it takes just another 2.6 seconds for that viewer's eyes to concentrate in a way that reinforces that first impression.

IT TAKES LESS THAN TWO-TENTHS OF A SECOND TO FORM AN OPINION

Whew! Talk about pressure! But there are some indicators that will help you and your team to work on the elements that are the most viewed in those first seconds.

The researchers employed eye-tracking software and an infrared camera to monitor study participants' eye movements as they perused the test website pages. Analysis of this eye movement helps to determine how long people focus on specific portions of a web page before moving on to another part of the page.

These are the results in order of time spent. Note that between the first item and the seventh, there was only a difference of about 1.23 seconds so all are pretty equally important: logos; navigation menus; search box; links to social utilities; primary image; written content; bottom of the page.

Participants were also asked to rate sites on the basis of their visual appeal and design and the same areas garnered the most interest and evaluation.

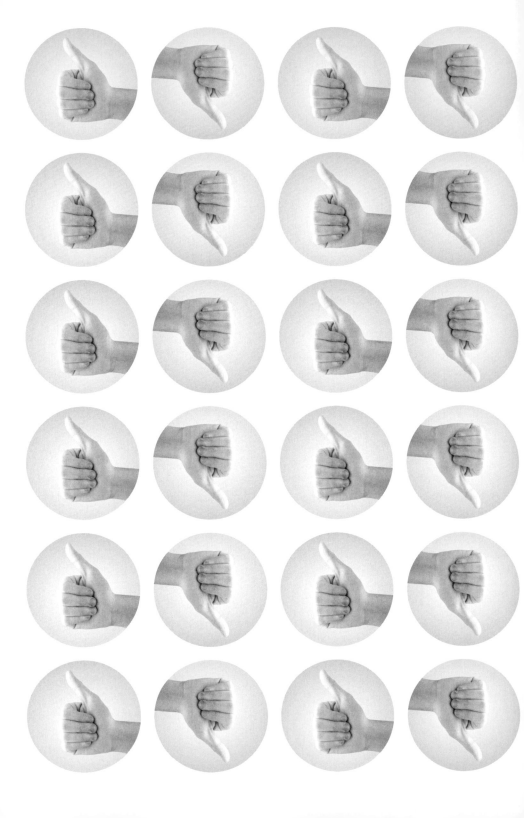

REALITY IS PERCEPTION

The reality of your brand is a combination of what you put out there about yourself and the experiences of your customers in their interactions with your brand. Both are about equally important. A customer may take your word for who you are or how you operate or identify with the image that you project of yourself on the first time around, but the results of that experience will serve to alter their perceptions, either favorably or unfavorably, moving forward.

Expensive advertising cannot compensate for weak brands, undifferentiated products or, especially, poor customer experience. Even so, less than 20% of companies have well-developed customer experience strategies (Econsultancy), and only 8% of companies deliver a truly superior customer experience (Bain & Company Survey).

Leaders in the field of customer experience include these imperatives in formulating their strategies:

- Design the right experience-focused value proposition for each segment of your target market.
- Delivering a consistent value proposition requires cross-functional collaboration of everyone in the company.
- Put systems in place to deliver the highest quality experience over and over again.
- Never stop trying to improve the experience; innovate.
- Define the customer experience and keep it consistent across all touch points in the company—sales, service, support, billing, shipping, etc.
- Own the issues. Be a part of the solution.
- Understand individual customer needs and work backwards to create an experience that exceeds expectations.

COMMUNICATION DESIGN

The AIGA (American Institute of Graphic Artists) states that graphic design, also known as communication design, is the art and practice of planning and projecting ideas and experiences with visual and textual content. The form of the communication can be physical or virtual, and may include images, words or graphic forms. The experience can take place in an instant or over a long period of time. The work can happen at any scale, from the design of a single postage stamp to a national postal signage system, or from a company's digital avatar to the sprawling and interlinked digital and physical content of an international newspaper. It can also be for any purpose, whether commercial, educational, cultural, or political.

DESIGN IS NOT JUST WHAT IT LOOKS LIKE. DESIGN IS HOW IT WORKS — STEVE J

My background and training stem from communication design. Educated in a pre-digital classic design curriculum, I learned the trade of traditional design. I also served as the President of the Art Directors and Designers Association. What I learned then is very different from what I do now—with two exceptions. The art is the same—communication—as is the challenge—how to build communication channels that fulfill a purpose and provide a unique experience.

If your goal is differentiation and competitive advantage, design thinkers are involved in creating ideas, not just dressing them up. More and more products and services we see today are the result of communication design—blending creative concepts about how the product should look, feel and work, and then shaping, designing and crafting the final form to meet a strategic marketing and sales plan. The resulting products and services creatively fill the needs and desires of their target customer groups.

Steve Jobs once said, "Design is not just what it looks like and feels like. Design is how it works." This doesn't imply that functionality is less important in strategic planning, but in the marketplace today when a consumer has a choice between two products of equal functionality, the aesthetics of the design can be the deciding factor in a purchase.

As the marketplace changes, and as consumers' needs and preferences change, the process of communication design will generate new and more effective ways to design and market products and services. If we look at current trends as indicators, we can make a few assumptions: customization and individualization of overall product design and features will continue to be an influence, as will ecologically oriented or "green" products and services, and products that tie in to social issues. In all cases, consumers and their satisfaction levels and needs will fuel the future of new creative directions and approaches to delivering tomorrow's products and services.

LOOK AT YOUR BRAND ON EVERY CHANNEL— IS THE BRAND CONSISTENT? WHEN YOU SEE AN AD, WATCH A VIDEO, TALK TO A CUSTOMER SERVICE REP, LIKE ON FACEBOOK—IS THE BRAND EXPERIENCE AND QUALITY THE SAME?

BRAND CONSISTENCY

	Consistency	Quality
Brand Visual Identity:		
Logo	① ② ③ ④ ⑤	① ② ③ ④ ⑤
Website	① ② ③ ④ ⑤	① ② ③ ④ ⑤
Social Media Channels	① ② ③ ④ ⑤	① ② ③ ④ ⑤
Marketing Materials	① ② ③ ④ ⑤	① ② ③ ④ ⑤
Buildings/Workspace	① ② ③ ④ ⑤	① ② ③ ④ ⑤
Promotional Items	① ② ③ ④ ⑤	① ② ③ ④ ⑤
Advertising	① ② ③ ④ ⑤	① ② ③ ④ ⑤
Sales Collaterals	① ② ③ ④ ⑤	① ② ③ ④ ⑤
Video/Animation	① ② ③ ④ ⑤	① ② ③ ④ ⑤
Customer Experience	① ② ③ ④ ⑤	① ② ③ ④ ⑤
Other: _____	① ② ③ ④ ⑤	① ② ③ ④ ⑤

Total Rating Points

Overall Evaluation**

· ·

Brand Consistency Exercise: **4.0+ Excellent; 3.5 good; 3.0 marginally okay; 2.5 needs much improvement; 2.0 badly hurting business. Ratings: 1=lowest; 5=highest.

· ·

BRAND PERCEPTION

HOW DOES THE WORLD PERCEIVE YOUR BRAND? (ACTUAL)

HOW DO YOU WANT THE WORLD TO PERCEIVE YOUR BRAND? (IDEAL)

Brand Perception Exercise: Ask both questions. Identify the significant differences, and brainstorm ways to align them.

WHO DO YOU MOST ADMIRE?

INDUSTRY LEADERS:

BRAND INFLUENCERS:

Who Do You Most Admire Exercise: Look at the leaders in your industry and other influential brands (or inspirational ones). What about them (from a first impression approach) might appeal to a prospect? What do you admire? What can you learn and/or bring to your brand strategy?

WHAT DO YOU SEE?

WHAT DO YOU SEE?

. . . .

Rorschach Inkblot Test: To introduce the concept that we all
see things differently, share this Rorschach inkblot test. This is a
psychological test in which subjects' perceptions of inkblots are
analyzed using interpretation and complex algorithms.
(Source: Rorschach test, Wikipedia)

. . . .

ARE YOU 'HONEST' WHEN YOU COMMUNICATE ABOUT YOUR BRAND AND PRODUCTS? DOES EVERYONE TELL THE SAME TRUE STORY?

THE ORGANIZATION'S MESSAGING IS CONSISTENT, TRUE, GENUINE AND COMMUNICATES VALUE PROPOSITIONS.

AUTHENTICITY

IDENTIFY WHERE YOU STAND.

Which of these statements most accurately reflects the current level of the organization's messaging?

- ☐ Our messaging is not clear.
- ☐ Our messaging is somewhat clear.
- ☐ Our messaging is clear, but not consistent.
- ☐ Our messaging is clear, consistent and genuine but it does not communicate our value propositions.
- ☐ Our messaging is clear, consistent and genuine and it communicates our value propositions.

WHEN WE DISCUSS AUTHENTICITY WE FOCUS ON MESSAGING. THAT'S BECAUSE YOU EXPRESS YOUR AUTHENTICITY THROUGH YOUR WORDS AND PROVE IT THROUGH YOUR ACTIONS. WHEN AN ORGANIZATION'S WORDS MATCH WHO IT IS AND WHAT IT BELIEVES AND ITS ACTIONS MATCH ITS WORDS, IT IS BEING AUTHENTIC. **START WITH THE QUESTION: "WHO ARE YOU?" YOUR COMPANY IS MADE UP OF LAYERS. TO TRULY BE AUTHENTIC, YOU MUST EXAMINE EACH OF THESE LAYERS UNTIL YOU REACH THE CORE OF YOUR BELIEFS, VISION AND GOALS.** THIS IS WHERE YOU FIND WHO YOU ARE AND WHAT YOU REPRESENT AS A COMPANY.

From there, every business decision you make should reflect who you are. Your authentic self is a collection of all of the things that make you and your business unique and individual—your passions, talents, inclinations, life experiences and especially your values and beliefs—what you stand for and why you're in the business you're in.

YOUR BRAND VOICE

Your brand voice is a combination of the tone of your communications, the particular words you choose and the style of writing and sentence structure that express the information you communicate.

A brand voice should be distinctive and recognizable—and an integral part of your overall brand identity. Consider for a moment the language we use everyday—both written and in speaking—and note how these have distinct differences. In speaking we use more colloquial, everyday words and expressions and more relaxed, less structured, and often run-on sentences. In writing, especially business writing, we tend to be more structured with sentences. They communicate complete thoughts and strive for clarity and simplicity to be better understood.

TONE OF VOICE IS AN EXTENSION OF YOUR PURPOSE

Everything begins with purpose in branding, even brand voice. That's because the voice expresses who and what you are—your values and your identity. Your voice, like your company's values, allows you to connect with your audience—to inform, engage, influence, persuade and build the relationship. You naturally choose words and ideas that your audience can understand and relate to.

Your brand voice combined with your visual identity strategy and company culture should be based on a coordinated brand strategy and work together to create a consistent and purposeful expression of your business.

Company culture is a compilation of the company vision, values, norms, systems, symbols, language, assumptions, beliefs, and habits. As such it's genetic, like DNA. Every company, even a sole proprietorship, has a culture. Employees don't bring culture to a company, the culture exists when they arrive. Since employees can impact the culture of a company for good or not so good, many companies try to make "fit" part of the overall hiring process. Equally important, once on board, is to educate employees on what the culture of the company is and how it is to be communicated.

Brand voice and social media voice—the differences.
Your corporate brand voice and social media voice both represent who you are as a business, but they are different. These voices and the personality they reflect help bring your brand to life. Here are some points that help describe the differences:

Brand Voice:
- Accurately reflects your brand personality
- Is a single, anonymous voice involved in one-way communication
- Is consistent across mediums
- Is unique to the organization

Social Voice:
- Involves a conversation between real people
- Reflects your brand as less formal and more human
- Is a two-way dialogue that's informative and engaging
- Listens, learns and responds

ARCHETYPAL BRANDS

Want to make your brand story characters more powerful and memorable? Find out what qualities of your main character (your business) are similar to those of well-known archetypes.

Archetypes are a concept developed by Swiss psychologist, Carl Jung. According to Jung, archetypes are elements, pictures or motifs within the collective unconscious of humanity—and he deduced their existence based on years of behavioral studies, dreams, and common symbols found within art, myths and religions worldwide.

Jung believed that in literature and films story characters can seem instantly familiar to us because elements of their personalities are primal and archetypal—a part of our shared collective unconscious. Archetypes represent a pattern of ideas that are timeless and symbolize basic human motivations, values and characteristics.

Some marketers believe that successful brands with a strong sense of identity may have an unconscious association, by consumers, with Jung's archetypal qualities. They claim that when a business identifies the archetype or archetypes that are most similar to its own personality, it can emphasize these aspects of its brand identity and personal story to create stronger unconscious appeal of its brand among potential customers.

They go further to claim that if a business also identifies complementary archetypal personalities among its potential prospects and mirrors the hopes and aspirations of those individuals through its marketing messages, it can potentially increase both its brand recognition and its top-of-mind awareness.

WHAT IS YOUR ARCHETYPAL PERSONALITY?

HERO	INNOCENT	CITIZEN	CAREGIVER
REBEL	MAGICIAN	SAGE	LOVER
CREATOR	JESTER	EXPLORER	SOVEREIGN

Instructions: Review the Brand Archetype descriptions with your team and identify your top 3. Look at your existing brand and find opportunities to bring your personality into your current brand.

BRAND ARCHETYPES

1. The Hero—also called the superhero or the warrior. The hero's desire is to prove its worth and leadership position. The core qualities of the hero include: quality, efficiency, reliability and being number one. Examples: Nike, The Avengers, Adidas, FedEx, Snickers, BMW.

2. The Innocent—also considered the romantic. Its core qualities are wholesome, pure, natural, safe, clean, free and happy. Examples: Dove soap, Ben & Jerry's ice cream, Red Cross, Coca Cola, Nintendo.

3. The Citizen—also called the everyman or the regular average guy. The qualities of this archetype are to belong, integrity, fairness, equity and responsibility to its community. Examples: Home Depot, Wendy's, Charles Schwab, Kit Kat bars, eBay, Trader Joes, Ikea.

4. The Caregiver—also called the parent, the nurturer or the altruist. The core qualities of this archetype are its unselfish concern and devotion to nurture and care for others. Examples: Johnson's Baby Shampoo, Mother Teresa, Campbell's Soups, The Salvation Army, UNICEF, Allstate Insurance, Heinz.

5. The Rebel—also called the outlaw or the revolutionary. The core qualities are change, being free-spirited, part of the counter-culture, brave and a rule breaker. Examples: Apple, PayPal, Virgin Industries (Richard Branson), E*Trade, Harley Davidson.

6. The Magician—also called the shaman or the visionary. The core qualities are a desire for the understanding of the universe and how it works. It is spiritual, holistic, and a visionary that sometimes works miracles. Examples: Disney, Dreamscape Multimedia, Oil of Olay, Victorinox/Swiss Army, Smirnoff.

7. The Sage—also called the scholar, the guru, the thinker, the philosopher or the teacher. The sage seeks truth and wisdom in all things. It is wise, open-minded, an expert, objective and autonomous, interested in substance over style and facts over speculation. Examples: BBC, CNN, Gallup, PBS, Smithsonian, Rosetta Stone, Oprah.

8. The Lover—also called the idealist or the dreamer. This archetype desires passion, sensuality, is indulgent in matters of the senses, and has a sexy sense of style. Examples: Godiva Chocolates, W Hotels, Chanel.

9. The Creator—also called the artist. The creator represents imagination, expressiveness, a willingness to take risks, is a cultural pioneer with a developed sense of the aesthetic. Examples: Lego, Sony, Crayola, Fast Company, Adobe, Google.

10. The Jester—also called the joker, the fool or the comedian. This archetype desires playfulness, spontaneity, is impulsive, fun, lives in the moment, is carefree and offers a unique perspective on truth and reality. Examples: M&Ms, GEICO, 7-UP.

11. The Explorer—also called the seeker or the wanderer. Its core qualities include a desire for adventure, excitement and discovery. It is self-directed, innovative, an individualist and a traveler. Examples: Jeep, REI, NASA, Patagonia, Corona, National Geographic.

12. The Sovereign—also called the ruler, the King or the Leader. Its desire is for power and control. It is decisive, stable, and enjoys being in charge. Examples: IBM, Microsoft, Consumer Reports, Brooks Brothers, British Airways.

The benefits of archetypal branding.

By identifying the archetype in your brand, theoretically you can amplify the impact of your brand by resonating with a familiar personality type in your audiences' unconscious. The archetype provides a guideline for how a brand can emphasize authentic qualities of itself to help it stand out and be recognized.

Brand archetypes are built on values and these values will resonate with both employees and customers. Shared values promote trust and build relationships over time. A trusted brand identity that represents a familiar archetype can potentially gain an advantage in creating top-of-mind awareness to grow and prosper.

"AUTHENTICITY IS OUR NATURAL STATE OF BEING. THE AUTHENTIC SELF IS A STATE OF BEING WHERE WE ARE CENTERED, CREATIVE, ADAPTIVE, AND INSPIRED." – HENNA INAM, WIRED FOR AUTHENTICITY

MESSAGING

What you say and how you say it represents what customers hear and what they think about you. Your message can either make you stand out or stay unnoticed among the competition.

M - "ME"

Share the personality of your business with your messaging.

E - ELEVATOR

Having an informative pitch helps others understand what your business does.

S - SIMPLIFY

Having a single message helps with consistency and clarity.

S - SINCERE

Be you. Don't allow messages to be sent out that do not represent you as an organization.

A - AUDIENCE

Be mindful of your target audience. Adjust to the audience you are talking to.

G - GET CONSISTENT

Make sure your messaging is consistent. Mixed messages can lead to mistrust with customers.

I - INTERNAL

Look within your company at your core values in order to develop messaging.

N - NEEDS

Speak to (and understand) what problems your ideal lead needs to solve.

G - GOOD

Get really good at presenting your value proposition. Practice. Practice. Practice.

STORYTELLING = "STORYSELLING"

Great stories have heroes. They have villains and they have conflict. They may have happy endings, sad endings or sometimes no ending at all. Bruce Springsteen, the Boss, has for decades painted pictures of the American experience through his music and lyrics. Each of his songs tells a story and these stories have the power to touch us as if he's talking about our lives, or someone we know.

Storytelling is as old as human communication. It's how lessons and news were communicated in days of old. Humans are hard-wired to listen to stories and learn from them. Great storytelling brings people together to share an experience, making one individual a part of something bigger. Then when you weave your product or service into the story, it simply has an accepted part in the action. It's the car that the hero drives; the instrument that the lead guitarist plays at the concert; the tool that the fireman uses to rescue the family from the burning building.

EVERY STORY YOU TELL CONTINUES TO BUILD THE VALUE OF YOUR COMPANY

Your brand, whether you know it or not, is made up of stories—your stories, your employees' stories and the stories others tell about you.

Your story is more than what you tell people, it's also what they believe about you based on their experience of interacting with your company. Your story is more than a catchy tagline. It's rooted in your own experience and your company's purpose (We keep coming back to that don't we?). This is why authenticity is such an important part of your story—what you say must ring true with your audience or you lose credibility and trust.

As Bruce Springsteen is to storytelling for entertainment, Steve Jobs is to storytelling for corporations. Jobs presented information to a corporate audience in an entertaining way—as a story. He was famous for his keynote addresses to announce new products and new innovations. What is not so well known is that he agonized for hours over the details of his presentations. And as a result, he delivered clear, inspiring messages and simple, bold ideas about technology and its ability to change lives.

HOW DO YOU TELL YOUR STORY?

One thing is certain—you can't expect to stand out from the crowd by telling the same story as everyone else. If you want to transform your organization, you first have to transform your story.

Your goal is to think differently about the stories you tell about your company. A good story is authentic, it's creative, intimate and emotional. It inspires action and takes the audience on a journey with the brand. Great stories affect the way we feel, the way we think and react and how we behave.

To tell your story, first know who you are or, more precisely, who your company is. Your story's main character (your business) has a personality. What's it like? Write down some of these qualities and create a personality profile to refer to and remember. Does your business personality have characteristics like any of the archetypes? Our main character is the "Twins." Our personality is made up of our separate strengths—creative, colorful, experimental, serious, analytic, rational. These qualities describe authentically who we are.

In the case of the "Life is Good" brand, their business personality didn't really click until they brought on board the brand character "Jake" as a representative of their products. Jake's smiling face became the brand protagonist for their story. His was the voice behind their statement that "Life is Good." It's this ongoing, overarching perspective of optimism that is the heart and soul of their brand story and what has built their success.

Identify who you are as a business—honestly, authentically and openly. Make the main character of your story someone that your customers can relate to and identify with—a character with similar values, goals and aspirations. Make them a part of your story and your storytelling can be transformed into storySelling.

CONSISTENCY BUILDS BRANDS

Another important thing we can learn from Steve Jobs is to maintain consistency in storytelling style. It's not just the words you speak, but how you look and how you project when you are telling your story. If you are the leader of an organization, your stories must align with the story of your organization. If they don't, there will be a disconnect and they will lack authenticity. An organization's story has to be genuine and it has to be you. And the style of your presentation must also be genuine, honest and reflect who you are, or it won't ring true.

"THE BEST BRANDS ARE BUILT ON GREAT STORIES." – IAN ROWDEN, VIRGIN GROUP

YOUR BRAND, WHETHER YOU KNOW IT OR NOT, IS MADE UP OF STORIES—YOUR STORIES, YOUR EMPLOYEES' STORIES AND THE STORIES OTHERS TELL ABOUT YOU. YOUR STORY IS MORE THAN WHAT YOU TELL PEOPLE, IT IS ALSO WHAT THEY BELIEVE ABOUT YOU BASED ON THEIR EXPERIENCE OF INTERACTING WITH YOUR COMPANY—IT'S ROOTED IN YOUR OWN EXPERIENCE AND WHO YOUR COMPANY IS.

CREATING A BRAND PERSONALITY

To make your brand story relevant and interesting, the characters in your story should reflect the personalities and social characteristics of your prospects and customers. Research that's available on marketing segments can identify very detailed qualities and activities of different consumers, providing valuable information on their lifestyles, habits, preferences, education, buying patterns, and even where they live.

With this detailed lifestyle data about your prospects, use characters in your brand story that will make psychological connections with your target audience. When your story messages and images can reflect the values, personality, and lifestyle preferences of your audience, they'll feel more involved with your brand. And ultimately their product or service becomes an obvious choice as an extension of your story.

The key to success with the storytelling strategy is authenticity— aligning what you communicate about your company, products or services with whom you truly are. If the personality a company attempts to portray is just a façade, a mask for what it truly is, then its storytelling attempts to create an appealing personality will eventually fail.

SO HOW CAN YOU MAKE YOUR BRAND MORE DISTINCT FROM THE COMPETITION?

The answer is simple. Tell the truth. Explain to customers who you are and what you stand for. Instead of trying to argue that your brand possesses certain aspects that they should consider important, show them what attributes you do have and let them decide.

By being honest, your company does not have to convince customers that it is something else. Most customers can spot "fake" brands from a mile away. And by authenticating your messaging, your company will stand out from the competition.

BRAND ATTRIBUTES

Take 15 minutes to write down the attritbutes that your existing customers would use to decribe your brand:

_____

_____

_____

_____

_____

_____

_____

BE PREPARED (TO TELL YOUR STORY)

Have you ever had that dream where you find yourself on center stage and can't remember your lines? Everyone is staring at you and recording everything you do. You're not prepared and the stage fright starts to take over.

In today's world, this nightmare often becomes a reality. Everything you say tells the story of your brand. There is a constant fear of never knowing who is recording what you say or when you say it. And once it is out there, you cannot take it back.

The only way to overcome this fear is to be prepared. When you're on that stage and in the spotlight, choose your words wisely and make sure those words are true.

To understand the importance of knowing what you stand for, try this. Step into an elevator and ask someone what they do. They will say something like "I am in business development for the XYZ Widget Company. We make widgets for businesses all over the state." Now ask them what they stand for. You will probably get silence and a shrug.

Picture yourself in this situation. You're in an elevator at a convention among your peers and someone asks, "What do you stand for?" What do you say? You've got about 15 seconds to establish yourself and make an impression. The person listening won't even be tuned in to the first 10 seconds because they are judging your appearance and their gut feeling about you. So, you've really got only five seconds. Can you say what you stand for in five seconds?

One one-thousand, two one-thousand, three one-thousand, four one-thousand, five one-thousand (and you're done).

ELEVATOR SPEECH

WHAT MAKES US DISTINCT:

ONE WORD:

_____
(Problem your product/service solves)

WE
_____
(Distinct advantage)

THAT
_____
(Key benefit)

UNIKE
_____
(The competition)

. . . .

Elevator Speech Exercise: Start with the structure – What client needs / What we provide / Where competitors don't. Then work in teams to apply the formula.

. . . .

AUTHENTICITY AND SOCIAL MEDIA

Social media has become one of the largest mediums for business communications in recent years. With hundreds of millions of monthly active users on Twitter and over a billion monthly active users on Facebook, companies are not only using social media as a way to communicate with their current customers, but also as a device to reach potential customers.

THE MESSAGE THAT LIVES ON AND ON...

"Blogs Will Change Your Business," was an article originally published in Businessweek magazine in 2005. Even though the article predated the splash of other social media venues like Twitter and Facebook, that original story is still being read, downloaded and linked to by thousands of people each month.

Businessweek editor Steve Baker says that if the article had been published in print, it would've gone into the recycling bin years ago. But because it was online, something strange happened. The more that people read and linked to the story, the higher the article rose in search engine rankings under the topic of "blogs."

As more people read and referred the article, its popularity snowballed. Bloomberg Business updated the article with new information about emerging social media and their impact on today's businesses. To continue to keep the story up to date, they're soliciting new facts and figures from their readers through their website. This one article, now more than ten years old, continues to live and grow in relevance.

This is the blessing and the curse of the online world. Once published, an article, a comment, a positive statement or criticism is always there for anyone to read. So choose your words carefully before you publish.

Social media represents an evolution in communications and an opportunity to build relationships unlike anything before. By using social media to broaden the distribution of your business communications, you are taking your message to where people can be reached more easily to connect.

The strategic use of social media venues can help you and your business:

• Connect with customers and prospects in ways that traditional advertising and public relations cannot.
• Deepen customer relationships.
• Develop and personalize your brand voice.

It's simply too important an opportunity to ignore. As a professional communicator and marketer, you can't afford to stand by quietly while others are shaping your brand reputation with their remarks or criticisms of your business.

. . . .

ONCE YOU, OR SOMEONE ELSE, PUBLISH AN ARTICLE, A COMMENT, A POSITIVE STATEMENT OR CRITICISM, IT WILL FOREVER BE THERE FOR SOMEONE TO READ. SO CHOOSE YOUR WORDS CAREFULLY.

. . . .

LOOK, LISTEN, LEARN

We know that social marketing is a two-way dialogue between the business and the audience. Integrating social media into your current marketing plan is like entering a preexisting conversation—people are already talking, possibly about you, and you can listen, talk back, steer the conversation, or start an entirely new one. Before entering, you should listen, to get a sense of what's already being said.

After this "listening" research, prepare a report that shows what you've found. This report can be presented to the leadership in your company, to show them what people are saying, and how social media can help guide these conversations towards what you want to "hear."

Now that you know what's already being said, set goals determining what you want to accomplish through the use of social media. What are your current communications objectives? What new ones would you like to accomplish? The key is to integrate social media into your marketing plan, not let it take over entirely. Each message that you post with social media should reflect your objectives and help you meet your goals.

To ensure visibility, you need to choose the right social networking sites for your communications. Each social media tool has something different to offer and is useful for different purposes. There are many options, so after some research on the benefits of each, make your selection, but also make sure you can explain the rationale for your choice.

HOW DO ONLINE COMMUNICATIONS FIT IN WITH YOUR OVERALL MESSAGING?

Your company's identity online is a large part of your brand's overall messaging strategy. People used to pick up the yellow pages to look for a business. Today, they use Google, Bing, Yahoo, or even Yelp to find information and reviews about businesses and their products and services.

But don't stop there. Search web forums and read comments containing what people are saying about your business, products, or services. Do your best to understand what they're saying and why they're saying it. Look at the situation as they would. What insights do you gain from this? If other members of your team have tried this same exercise, compile a list of everyone's insights and compare them. With the knowledge of these new insights, you can adjust your social marketing strategy or brand messaging so that others will see the best of your business.

"AFTER A PRESENTATION, 63% OF ATTENDEES REMEMBER STORIES. ONLY 5% REMEMBER STATISTICS." – CHIP & DAN HEATH

PROBLEM/SOLUTION

PROBLEMS WE SOLVE:	SOLUTIONS WE PROVIDE:
_____	_____
_____	_____
_____	_____
_____	_____
_____	_____
_____	_____
_____	_____
_____	_____
_____	_____

Problem/Solution Exercise: What problems do you solve? What solutions do you provide? Draw a line connecting each problem to a solution. Look for areas where they don't align.

BRAND DESCRIPTION

I	O		I	O	
		AGGRESSIVE			INTENSE
		AMBITIOUS			INNOVATIVE
		BOLD			INSPIRED
		BUSY			LOYAL
		CAPABLE			OPEN
		CARING			ORGANIZED
		COCKY			PASSIONATE
		COLD			PREDICTABLE
		CONSERVATIVE			RELIABLE
		CONFIDENT			REVOLUTIONARY
		CONFUSED			SINCERE
		CREATIVE			SMART
		DETERMINED			STRATEGIC
		EAGER			STRONG
		EFFECTIVE			SUCCESSFUL
		ENLIGHTENED			SUPERIOR
		ENTHUSIASTIC			SYSTEMATIC
		FORMAL			STRATEGIC
		GLAMOROUS			TRUSTWORTHY
		IMPRESSIVE			UNIQUE
		INFORMAL			VERSATILE

Brand Description Exercise: What four (4) words from the following list would you use to describe the brand of your organization? (place an X to the left of your top 4 for each - inside and outside). I = Inside the organization; O= Outide the organization

DO YOU **TARGET YOUR MARKETING** TO YOUR IDEAL LEAD

OR ARE YOU MARKETING TO EVERYONE IN THE SAME WAY?

HOW'S THAT WORKING?

THERE IS A CONSISTENT FUNNEL OF IDEAL LEADS THAT ARE DEFINED, NURTURED AND MANAGED.

....

IDEAL LEADS

....

IDENTIFY WHERE YOU STAND.

Which of these statements most accurately reflects your situation with generating consistent ideal leads?

- [ ] We do not have a consistent funnel of leads.
- [ ] We somewhat have a consistent funnel of leads.
- [ ] We have a consistent funnel of leads, but they are not segmented to our ideal lead.
- [ ] We have a consistent funnel of ideal leads and they are defined but they are not nurtured or managed.
- [ ] We have a consistent funnel of ideal leads and they are defined, nurtured and managed.

WHAT'S AN IDEAL LEAD? A PROSPECT WHO FITS YOUR DEFINED CUSTOMER PROFILE AND IS INTERESTED IN WHAT YOU HAVE TO OFFER. THIS PERSON SEES VALUE FROM USING YOUR PRODUCT OR SERVICE AND CAN APPRECIATE THE DIFFERENCES THAT YOUR PRODUCT OR SERVICE OFFERS COMPARED TO YOUR COMPETITORS.

Ideal leads are an issue of quality over quantity. For some organizations this may require a new perspective on leads. If the effectiveness of your lead generation process is based only on the number of leads your marketing team generates, then it's likely that there is a lot of time being wasted chasing leads that are not "ideal."

Get more from less. In actuality, bringing in fewer leads can result in more revenue and less time converting ideal leads into customers. Your sales team works best with leads that are a good fit for what you have to offer and there's a strong possibility that when presented with the right offer, the leads are ready and willing to make a decision.

Understanding who your ideal lead is and building a strategy to attract them will help improve the efficiency and productivity of your sales team. You can feed them fewer, higher quality leads and they'll do what they're best at—converting leads to sales.

Profile your current customers. A good place to begin in defining your ideal lead is to look at your existing customers. What things do they have in common? What in their demographics are similar and what are different? Add this information to your lead profile and expand from there. You may even ask your existing customers what attracted them to your product or service and what convinced them to buy.

THE IDEAL LEAD PROFILE

The first step to creating an ideal lead flow is to agree on a set of criteria of what an ideal lead looks like for your company, then develop a profile to better focus your sales and marketing team's efforts. The following are examples of information that you may include in your lead profile:

☐ **A set of demographics that includes job level and seniority.**

☐ **A day in their lives.**

☐ **A list of their pain points, motivations and goals.**

☐ **Where do they look for information?**

Your research will allow you to refine your ideal lead profiles over time and make it clear what qualities best identify your true prospects. Once you understand what your ideal leads look like and what motivates them you can develop content directed to them—information they are looking for to solve problems or overcome specific challenges. The more information you can provide, the more helpful you can be, the better. Providing them with useful information builds trust so that when they are ready to buy, you are top-of-mind. This is marketing through attraction; marketing through relationship building.

Once you establish a relationship, you are able to identify where a prospect is in your sales funnel model. This enables you to develop marketing messages that fit who they are and where they are in the process of becoming a customer.

This is where the skill of your marketing team comes in. You define the right prospect (ideal lead) and they develop the right message and the right offer to motivate a response.

YOUR SALES FUNNEL

Top of the Sales Funnel—People who don't know you. They are looking for information to solve a problem or meet a need. It's important that they perceive you as a source of information, to educate them so they are well-informed about the solutions available and have what they need to make a decision. Effective ways to communicate at this stage include: website content, blogs, customer reviews, social media, keywords, etc.

Middle of the Sales Funnel—These prospects are aware of your products and services and have shown some interest by communicating with you in some form. They might have searched your website, downloaded an eBook from your website, interacted with your team through social media or contacted you for additional information. Your opportunity is to provide the information they need in a way that nurtures and grows the relationship. Create a positive experience so they will choose your product or service over a competitor's.

Bottom of the Sales Funnel—These are ideal leads. They are ready to buy but haven't made a final decision. This is when having the right offer will motivate them to make a decision and close the sale.

Grow the relationship—The sale is just one step in building a long-term relationship. Once a lead becomes a customer, it's important to continue to nurture your relationship so you will be top-of-mind when they have additional needs or when they recommend your product or service to their peers.

"NURTURED LEADS MAKE 47% LARGER PURCHASES THAN NON-NURTURED LEADS" —THE ANNUITAS GROUP

LOVE THE LEADS YOU'RE WITH

It's important to give a lot of love to the relationships in your business world. A lot of what you do to nurture a personal relationship can be applied to business relationships. Online traffic that has been converted into leads needs "love" and nurturing, just like any other relationship. What can you do to love your leads and convert them into new sales?

Check out this list of best practices:

Know your leads. Different campaigns draw in different leads. When you develop campaigns to send to your leads, tailor each to specific groups. Don't lump all of your leads together.

Deliver what you promise. What was your initial offer to your leads? If you promised something by a specific date, then have it ready for them by that date. If you did not include a specific timeline, have their offer ready in a reasonable amount of time. Don't keep your leads waiting.

Be accessible and available. Your leads may have questions or want more information before they make a buying decision. You, or someone in your business, needs to be accessible to them, through email or phone, with answers. When creating a new campaign, hold a meeting with whatever departments in your business will be involved to get everyone on the same page. Everyone should know how to handle situations when leads have questions.

Schedule regular interactions. Much like a weekly or monthly date night, your leads need to have a regularly scheduled interaction with you, whether it's through email, a phone call, or something else. Determine a "balanced" schedule of these interactions that shows consistency, but doesn't overwhelm your leads with a barrage of constant communication. **Be unique and valuable.** What can you offer your leads that they can't get anywhere else? What offer can you provide that holds value for them? The more unique and valuable your offers are, the more reasons your leads will have to check back and continue a relationship with you.

CLASSIFYING YOUR LEADS

Preferred passenger—This is an ideal lead, someone who fits with your company's values and product / service offering. They have the potential of becoming a healthy two-way relationship (you provide value to them and they provide value to you through loyalty and referrals). You want to spend most of your time focusing on these leads.

Frequent flyers—These are your long-term relationships (and also preferred passengers). They are loyal. They need to be nurtured.

Stowaways—These individuals are high maintenance. They require more of your energy and attention and offer low value to your organization.

Cargo—These leads weigh your business down. Interacting with them can negatively impact the culture of your company and be a drag on your operations. They're not profitable and should be jettisoned.

STRANGERS TO PROMOTERS

This funnel illustrates how inbound marketing can turn strangers into promoters. It illustrates the most effective digital marketing activities to attract strangers, convert visitors to leads, leads to customers and then customers to raving fans. Rather than sending out marketing messages in hopes that someone is interested in what you have to say, these activities deliver information where your ideal lead is looking to help them solve a problem. Once they are in your funnel you can customize content based on their specific needs and wants. *(Original source: HubSpot)*

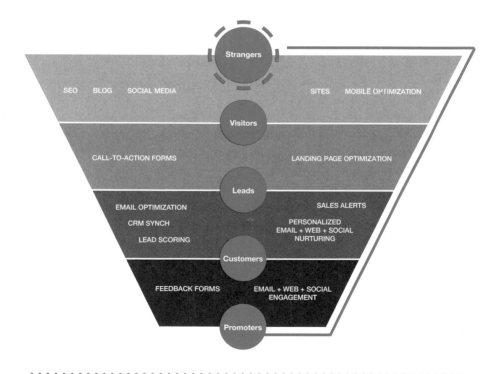

"EVERYONE IS NOT YOUR CUSTOMER." — SETH GODIN

IDEAL LEAD BRAINSTORM

WHO ARE THEY:

WHERE ARE THEY:

WHAT'S IMPORTANT TO THEM:

WHAT KEEPS THEM UP AT NIGHT:

Ideal Lead Brainstorm: Brainstorm with the team to understand ideal lead roles, motivations and challenges they face professionally and personally.

IDEAL LEAD PERSONA MAP

NAME:

ROLE AND TENURE:

KEY ISSUES AND RESPONSIBILITIES:

PERSONAL PROFILE:

WHAT MAKES
JOB HARD?

WHAT MAKES
JOB FUN?

Ideal Lead Persona Map: Create a map for each persona. (You should ultimately have one Ideal Lead and several personas).

CLOSING THE SALE

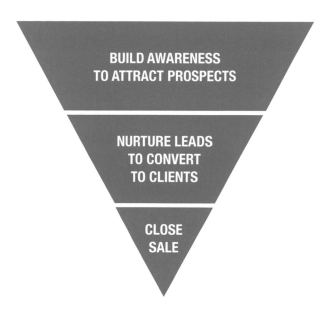

BUILDING AWARENESS:

NURTURING LEADS:

Closing the Sale Exercise: What specific things are you doing to lead to and support the closing of a sale? Record specific actions/initiatives for building awareness and nurturing leads.

IF WE FOCUS ON WHAT MAKES EACH OF US DISTINCT,

PROSPECTS WOULD NOT BE CONFUSED BY EVERYTHING

LOOKING THE SAME.

STANDS OUT AMONG ITS COMPETITORS, INFLUENCERS AND INDUSTRY THOUGHT LEADERS.

DISTINCTION

IDENTIFY WHERE YOU STAND.

Which of these statements most accurately reflects the current level that your organization stands out among its competitors, influencers and industry thought leaders?

- ☐ We do not stand out.
- ☐ We are not clear on how we stand out.
- ☐ We stand out but we do not consistently communicate why and how we stand out.
- ☐ We stand out among our competitors, but we do not stand out to outside influencers and industry thought leaders.
- ☐ We stand out among our competitors, influencers and industry thought leaders.

DISTINCTION: DIFFERENCE OR CONTRAST BETWEEN SIMILAR THINGS OR PEOPLE; POSITIVE QUALITIES THAT SET A BUSINESS APART FROM OTHERS. THE SECRET TO GAINING DISTINCTION IS TO INFLUENCE PROSPECTS BY BEING WHO YOU ARE, OPERATING FROM A FOUNDATION BASED ON PURPOSE, AND WORKING FROM A POSITION OF CONFIDENCE ABOUT WHAT DIFFERENCE YOU CAN MAKE IN PEOPLE'S LIVES. HOW CAN YOU ACCOMPLISH THIS?

When Lorrie and I were children, each morning our mother would lay out our clothes on a green "pleather" chair in our living room. You know those plastic leather chairs that were popular back in the 70s? The ones that if you fell asleep on them, your face would stick to the fake leather? Well, each morning we'd get up and get dressed for school and our outfits for the day would be sitting on that green chair and always they were exactly alike.

I never could figure out why she dressed us the same. But as a result, most people knew us as the "little twins." I guess it was considered cute. They would say, "Look, there go the little twins." They didn't even know our names, only that we were twins.

Our grandmother made most of our clothes, so maybe it was easier to simply make two sets of everything rather than sewing separate things for the two of us. Maybe they didn't want to show any preference for either one by picking out different clothes. Maybe it was their way of emphasizing the special relationship that twins share. I'm not sure, but I can say with certainty that it makes it very hard to stand out and be noticed as an individual when you always look exactly like somebody else.

I didn't think about it much until I was almost 13. Around that time, I remember clearly that looking and being different from my twin sister was just about the most important thing in my world. I wanted to be seen as a separate and distinct person. And when you've been one-half of the little twins for 13 years, you have to make some pretty dramatic changes to alter that perception.

So that's what I did. I dressed as differently as I could, which back in those days meant I wore black a lot. I cut my hair differently, I hung out with other people who were trying to be different, too—artists, musicians and other experimental types who for one reason or another were trying to find their own identities. What I found was that most of what I did to be different was external. I was trading being part of one group (the twins) with being part of another, larger group (creative types).

Most of us want to be recognized for our differences—the unique qualities that make us special and help us stand out from everyone else. It took me many years of trying to be something or someone else before I learned the important truth that the shortest course to being different is to be more of who I am.

SPOT THE DIFFERENCE

Distinction Exercise: Can you spot the differences that make these similar images distinct one from the other? Top: identical twins Center: manipulated images Bottom: counterfeit coins

YOUR MOST DISTINGUISHING CHARACTERISTICS

Identifying the characteristics that distinguish a company from its competitors has never been more essential for success than it is now. The Internet and global media have drawn every industry in to international focus. With these changes come expanded opportunities as well as expanded exposure. If a company does not tell its own story, someone else will create it for them.

In the process of standing out, you learn to define and communicate your purpose (who you are) and what you stand for. And you make your purpose a focus of your marketing efforts and messaging (what you do). Next you explore your brand personality to find out which parts best represent the strengths and memorable qualities of the main character of your brand story (your company). All of these steps can establish and direct how your business can become noticed, remembered and distinguished in the marketplace.

WHAT CHARACTERISTIC IS UNIQUE TO YOU THAT YOU CAN LEVERAGE TO BUILD YOUR BRAND TO STAND OUT?

YOUR DISTINCT ADVANTAGE IS NOT JUST WHAT MAKES YOUR PRODUCT OR SERVICE DIFFERENT, IT'S WHAT MAKES YOUR COMPANY DIFFERENT — AND WHAT YOUR COMPANY STANDS FOR AND WHY ITS IN BUSINESS. IT IS THE UNIQUE COMBINATION OF GIFTS, EXPERIENCES, CULTURE, STORIES, SKILLS AND INCLINATIONS THAT MAKE UP WHO YOU ARE AND WHAT YOU DO IN WAYS THAT YOUR COMPETITION DOESN'T, CAN'T AND WON'T.

AUTHENTICITY AND YOUR DISTINCT ADVANTAGE

In the process of creating communications (marketing messages) about its products or services, it's typical for a company to overlook "authenticity" in favor of things that they believe are more attention grabbing—flashy product features, showy design elements and clever messages. And yet authenticity is the very thing that helps build relationships and keep customers coming back again and again.

Under the Brand Traffic Control process, those things that authentically distinguish a company from its competitors will have greater clarity and alignment to its vision, it's values and beliefs and its purpose. When a company aligns its operations and activities with its purpose and its authentic personality, it operates from a position of confidence and strength.

Your distinct advantage is not just what makes your product or service different, it's what makes your company different. Identifying your purpose—why you do what you do and what difference that makes to your customers—takes some soul searching to pin down, but it is worth the effort. Companies which used to have one or two local competitors could now have dozens or even hundreds of competitors in the online marketplace which the Internet has created.

Ultimately distinct advantage is where what you offer aligns with the distinct needs of your prospects and customers in a place where your competitors don't, can't or won't. Instead of trying to be all things to all people, your purpose and your distinct advantage help you and your business get "pointy"—more focused on who you are and what you're in business to do.

INSTEAD OF TRYING TO BE ALL THINGS TO ALL PEOPLE, YOUR PURPOSE AND YOUR DISTINCT ADVANTAGE HELP YOU AND YOUR BUSINESS GET "POINTY" ON WHO YOU ARE AND WHAT YOU'RE IN BUSINESS TO DO.

When you say, "this is what we stand for and this is why we do what we do"—you do so with the understanding that you will appeal most to those people who share your values and who relate to what you say you stand for. But that's okay, because those people are your ideal prospects—your ideal leads and ultimately your brand ambassadors.

DISTINGUISH YOUR COMPANY. BECOME A THOUGHT LEADER.

When you create consistent and genuine messaging throughout your company and align your messaging with your company's core values, beliefs, and purpose you will stand out and take off. Having a great product or service is not enough to distinguish your company in the marketplace today—and advertising alone won't get the attention and loyalty of customers to support sustained growth.

You are a leader of your company and leaders think like leaders, not like followers. To distinguish yourself from the crowd, take the next step and become a thought leader in your industry.

Imagine that your purpose is a verb instead of a noun. Standing for something is great, but acting with purpose and sharing your views can turn a good company into a great company and change your industry and the world.

Make your words and actions an authentic reflection of who you are and what you believe and you'll naturally find your groove, hit your stride, and achieve maximum efficiency and impact. When a company is being true to itself, true to its values and beliefs, and true to the reasons for its own existence, it's in a position to harness the full potential of its people and resources.

To become a thought leader, share your thoughts, your views and opinions about your business and your industry—in writing, through publishing in industry publications and through speaking at industry events. Start small and gain practice.

By speaking and writing about your business and what you're doing that's different or distinct, you'll become even more familiar with your own uniqueness and you may even inspire others to be more of who they are. Pay attention to how others react and respond to your message as well. You may get important new ideas for further growth and development from the comments of your audience.

WHAT DO YOU WANT TO BE KNOWN FOR?

To identify your distinct advantage, look beyond what you sell to how you sell it and "what you want to be known for." This last quality is your "stake in the ground" i.e., this is what we do and we do it better because we believe it will make our customers' lives better, provide convenience in their busy day, make them feel happier and live fuller lives. Well, maybe your product or service won't do all of those things, but you get the picture.

Let's look at some examples to clarify this concept of distinct advantage.

Zappos—At the heart of their success is the goal to provide the best customer service that their customers had ever received—to deliver a "Wow" experience of service that their customers wouldn't forget. Their product was simple: shoes, purchased online, delivered without charge and if the customer wasn't happy, Zappos would pay for return of the shoes as well. The company didn't just sell shoes, they sold "happiness" and customer satisfaction.

While some marketers focus on things like return on investment, maximizing profitability, product innovation, and beating the competition, Zappos focuses on customer service. It's how they've built their brand and it's how they've built an extraordinary employee culture as well to support the extraordinary service they deliver. Happy employees = service with a smile. The company even takes much of the money it might spend on advertising and invests it in customer service—building on its strength.

Starbucks—A simple idea was behind the success of Starbucks. Based on the example of the Italian coffee drinking culture and neighborhood coffeehouses, Starbucks CEO Howard Shultz had the idea to make good coffee easily accessible through a network of neighborhood coffeehouses. Their purpose is not to sell coffee, but "to inspire and nurture the human spirit—one person, one cup and one neighborhood at a time."

From early experience as a neighborhood coffee shop in Seattle, they learned that their customers preferred quality premium coffee in a comfortable and convenient location. Based on this vision, as the demand for specialty coffee, cappuccinos and lattes began to grow, so did Starbucks. Quality coffee, convenient location, with a personality that was distinct and friendly.

Uber—Who could have imagined someone finding a niche in the venerable, but rather uninteresting, world of taxi service? Enter mobile technology and the creators of Uber, who in 2009, saw a way to evolve the way the world moves by seamlessly connecting riders to drivers through mobile apps. Within six years, the company is bringing people and their destinations closer in 300 cities in 58 countries and is estimated to be worth 50 billion dollars.

Home Depot—Remember the neighborhood hardware store? In 1978, that industry was transformed with a breakthrough idea—one-stop shopping for the do-it-yourselfer. The concept has revolutionized the home improvement industry by bringing tools and know-how directly to consumers, saving them money. Since duplicated, but still going strong, The Home Depot brand ranks #37 on Forbes list of the 100 Most Valuable Brands and #134 on the Global 2000 List.

Facebook—Founded in 2004, this online social networking service is estimated to have 1.44 billion active monthly users. Its goal is simple and brilliant: give people the power to share and make the world more open and connected; celebrate friendship and how our friends inspire us, support us and help us discover the world when we connect. Are you on Facebook?

Houzz—Houzz is an online platform for home remodeling and design, bringing homeowners and home professionals together in a uniquely visual community. It is also a place to connect with other homeowners and home design enthusiasts from around the world.

Tesla—Tesla Motors, Inc. is an American automotive and energy storage company that designs, manufactures, and sells luxury electric cars, electric vehicle powertrain components, and battery products. Its founders are a group of Silicon Valley engineers who are out to prove that electric cars can be better than gasoline-powered ones, and more ecologically sustainable.

iOffice—iOffice is a workplace managment solution provider. They believe that great companies are defined by the results of their high-performing teams. True leaders create the environments where their people can thrive. The power of the workplace lies in the people who bring it to life, and by giving them technology that's easy, smart and works like they do—mobile, configurable, and open – they give people the tools they need to move mountains, not just manage them.

Livestream—Livestream is an online platform that enables the broadcast and viewing of live events. Its goal is to democratize live video broadcasting and to provide the tools to make any event live online. It is estimated that 40,000,000 + viewers watch events every month via the website or downloadable apps.

"YOUR BRAND IS WHAT OTHER PEOPLE SAY ABOUT YOU WHEN YOU'RE NOT IN THE ROOM."
— JEFF BEZOS, AMAZON

DISTINCT ADVANTAGE WORKSHEET

WHAT CLIENTS WANT:

WHAT YOU PROVIDE:

WHAT COMPETITORS OFFER:

Distinct Advantage Worksheet: What do your ideal clients want that you provide and your competitors don't? Use findings to identify your distinct advantages in this section.

DISTINCT ADVANTAGE

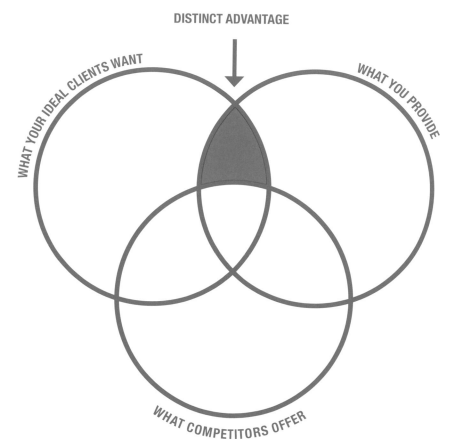

DISTINCT ADVANTAGE

WHAT YOUR IDEAL CLIENTS WANT

WHAT YOU PROVIDE

WHAT COMPETITORS OFFER

Distinct Advantage Exercise: What do your ideal clients want that you provide and your competitors don't? Use findings from the Distinct Advantage Worksheet.

DISTINCT ADVANTAGE SUMMARY

DISTINCT ADVANTAGES:

PRIMARY DISTINCT ADVANTAGE:

DISTINCT ADVANTAGE STATEMENT:

Distinct Advantage Summary: Summarize the results here. Your distinct advantage statement will serve as a component for your Elevator Speech in the Authenticity section.

DISTINCT ADVANTAGE MESSAGING

PRIMARY MESSAGES:

RECURRING MESSAGES:

Distinct Advantage Messaging: Summarize the results here.
Messaging is the content that is a result of distinct advantage activity
and findings.

WITH THOUSANDS OF WAYS TO COMMUNICATE TODAY,
THE KEY IS ALIGNING COMMUNICATIONS AND MARKETING IN A WAY THAT
ACHIEVES BUSINESS GOALS.

A 12-MONTH MARKETING STRATEGY IS IN FORCE AND ALIGNED WITH THE ORGANIZATION'S GOALS

. . . .

STRATEGY

. . . .

IDENTIFY WHERE YOU STAND.

Which of these statements most accurately reflects the current level of your organization's 12-month marketing plan?

☐ We have no marketing plan.

☐ We somewhat have a marketing plan

☐ We have a 12-month marketing plan that is in force, but it is not aligned with our organization's goals.

☐ We have a 12-month marketing plan that is aligned with our business goals but is not implemented consistently.

☐ We have a 12-month marketing plan that is in force, implemented consistently and aligned with our organization's goals.

STRATEGY INVOLVES A COMMITMENT BY YOUR ENTIRE TEAM TO AN INTEGRATED SET OF GOALS AND ACTIONS ACROSS YOUR ORGANIZATION. YOUR SALES, MARKETING, COMMUNICATIONS AND BRAND STRATEGIES SHOULD SYNC TOGETHER AND SUPPORT ONE ANOTHER. INTEGRATED STRATEGIES PROMOTE ALIGNMENT, CLARIFY OBJECTIVES AND PRIORITIES AND FOCUS ALL OF YOUR EFFORTS TOWARD THE SAME GOALS.

When your business strategy is aligned with your purpose and brand, you are on course to achieve your company goals. Under the traditional business model, business strategies and marketing strategies were often separate and did not always interact or support one other. Ideally, when a company is working from its purpose, marketing and business strategies work hand-in-hand. Like purpose, they are integrated and communicated across the entire organization. When companies invest the time to align their brand, strategy and purpose, they build the foundation for successfully staying on course. And when strategy and purpose are combined in a written strategic plan, then a company can truly take off.

CREATE A PLAN

While formulating and adjusting strategy is an ongoing requirement of good management, it will be wasted effort without a plan that defines the steps and actions needed to accomplish the goals and to orchestrate their implementation.

Even so, many companies do not spend the time required on the front end to schedule initiatives, assign roles and accountability and set up interim check-ins to determine how the plans are evolving toward completion. While long-term strategy may be fluid and subject to such things as market and price changes, the entry of new competitors into the market and even innovations, short-term initiatives can provide the flexibility to accommodate change while achieving interim objectives.

PUT IT IN WRITING

When you put your plan in writing, you can refer to it later and use it as a baseline from which you can measure progress. If it's not written down, you can forget steps or parts that are crucial to where you want to go.

ASSIGN RESPONSIBILITY

Let every team member know what role they will play in the overall plan. Explain the tasks they're expected to perform and when they're expected to complete them (due dates). When team members have a clear picture of their task and when they need to complete it, when they're motivated by a shared purpose and a common goal, the entire team will work more efficiently and effectively.

YOU ARE ON COURSE WHEN PURPOSE IS IN ALIGNMENT WITH BRAND AND STRATEGY

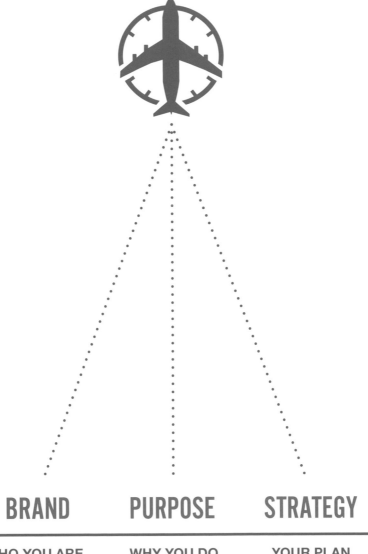

BRAND **PURPOSE** **STRATEGY**

WHO YOU ARE WHY YOU DO
WHAT YOU DO YOUR PLAN
OF ACTION

CREATIVE + STRATEGY = HYBRID THINKING

Being twins, we're convinced that two heads and two brains are better than one. And we use the term "hybrid thinking" to describe the blending of creative thinking and strategic thinking that we bring to the table when discussing solutions for our clients. Conversations are no longer about whether a brochure should be blue or green, but about who's the target audience? What are their needs, and what's the best way to reach them?

For years, design was considered a down-stream aspect of business and marketing processes. A product or service would be developed to fill a perceived market need. Then in the final stages, the designer would be called in to create an "attractive package" to make it more appealing to consumers - the visuality of the brand. But today the creative thinking process goes beyond the visual identity of a brand. According to Tim Brown, the president and CEO of the creative consulting firm IDEO, "... today, if you are developing a marketing strategy, building a new retail space, streamlining a manufacturing operation, or creating a marketing plan to introduce or promote a product or service, your planning is influenced and enhanced by creative thinking." In a presentation to MIT Sloan business students about design and innovation, Brown explained that the creative thinking process is applicable to a wide range of business challenges, "from products to services to spaces."

More and more products and services we see today are the result of mixing creativity and strategy into a more unified and innovative approach to developing and marketing products and services. It's a hybrid: 50% creative + 50% strategic = 100% effective. This right brain (creative) and left brain (strategic) approach to marketing and design blends creative concepts about how the product should look, feel and work, and then shapes, designs and crafts the final form into a strategic marketing plan that fills the needs and desires of target consumer groups.

Brown states that design thinking adds a "human-centered" approach to problem solving. It considers the real needs and wants of people and factors these into the way products and services are created, packaged, marketed, supported and serviced. Traditional business thinking ordinarily relies on feature- or function-driven models. Design thinking considers the consumer's feelings of satisfaction about the way a product or service fulfills their needs and is an integral part of a customer-focused brand strategy.

Design differentiates. It distinguishes the look and feel of a product or company as well as the values and personality behind it. Design reflects a company's personality and thinking, and in today's world, consumers choose products and services that mirror their own values, personalities and lifestyles. Design influences consumers' buying decisions and is a source of competitive advantage that positively impacts a company's earnings.

"DESIGN IS THE METHOD OF PUTTING FORM AND CONTENT TOGETHER. DESIGN, HAS MULTIPLE DEFINITIONS; THERE IS NO SINGLE DEFINITION. DESIGN CAN BE ART. DESIGN CAN BE AESTHETICS. DESIGN IS SO SIMPLE, THAT'S WHY IT'S SO COMPLICATED."– PAUL RAND

STRATEGIC THINKING

Strategic thinking is simply a matter of seeing through your CEO's and CFO's eyes. According to Susanne Lyons, former Chief Marketing Officer at Visa and Charles Schwab, "CEOs and CFOs think in terms of profitability, cash flow, and revenue. When you plan for the coming year, think of the impact your marketing activities will have on generating revenue for your company. Then communicate your marketing programs using terms that resonate with the goals of your senior executives." By thinking and acting strategically, you show that you understand how your marketing activities contribute to your company's bottom-line growth. You demonstrate that you can leverage your marketing and advertising budget to improve your company's financial health.

Listen to your customers – Listen to your customers more closely. Survey or interview them to learn why they feel your product is important. Learn what they like and dislike. What you learn could help improve the way you market and even show you the type of new customer prospects to look for. In the process, you may gather positive client comments and testimonials that can help build credibility for marketing to new prospects.

According to Steve Strauss, Money columnist for USA Today, "Selling is not manipulation. It's a process whereby you discover a potential customer's needs and then show them that your product or service fills that need better than your competition." Your current customers are your best prospects. Thank them for their business, reward them for their loyalty and they'll keep coming back. Tom Peters, well-known writer and lecturer on excellence in business practices, says, "The magic formula that successful businesses have discovered is to treat customers like guests and employees like people."

See yourself through your customer's eyes – Take a fresh look this year at your product or service – from your customer's perspective. Think less about why you feel your product or service is special, and more about what your customer feels is important. What are your product's real strengths? What are its benefits in the eyes of your customer? Benefits describe how your product or service improves a person's life. Benefits include convenience, ease, and saving time and money. Benefits say how your product satisfies real customer needs and desires. They are emotion-based. According to the website, entrepreneur.com, benefits answer your customer's question "What's in it for me?" Does your marketing message identify what's in it for your customers? Make sure you spell out the benefits in all your communications.

"GOOD STRATEGIES PROMOTE ALIGNMENT, CLARIFY OBJECTIVES AND PRIORITIES AND HELP FOCUS EFFORTS—A COMMITMENT TO A SET OF COHERENT, MUTUALLY REINFORCING BEHAVIORS AIMED AT ACHIEVING SPECIFIC, COMPETITIVE GOALS. " – HBR.COM

WHY PLANNING MATTERS

Think about how many times you use the word "plan" in your day. "I plan on doing (blank)." "Our plans include…" "What are you planning for (blank)?" We use the word so much that many people forget the importance of the actions required to bring the plan to life.

Challenges occur in every industry. Wouldn't you rather be prepared for them? By creating a plan, you can respond to challenges that arise in real time. When developing your plan it's important to include "what-if" scenarios. Stuff happens—things that are unexpected such as ups and downs in the market or the economy, changes in industry standards and environmental factors.

YOUR LEVEL OF PERFORMANCE DEPENDS ON YOUR LEVEL OF PREPAREDNESS

Planning ahead gives you time to adjust your plan on your schedule and at your convenience rather than frantically altering your plan to adapt to changing circumstances. Updating and revising your plan regularly is important.

Your level of performance depends on your level of preparedness. Through planning, you are able to see what next steps should be taken in your business and make adjustments to stay on course.

Planning empowers you to:

- Be proactive
- Have time to adjust
- Improve performance

PLANNING FOR THE FUTURE

Who knows what the future will bring and how we should plan for it? In 1994, who could have known how big the Internet was going to become? Now more than 20 years later, most of our lives and jobs revolve around the Internet. In fact, The Today Show's Bryant Gumbel and Katie Couric contemplated the Internet during one of their 1994 programs. They questioned what the '@' symbol stood for and what exactly the Internet was.

In a memorable Super Bowl ad, BMW suggested that, while the future is scary, new ideas take some time getting used to. Thanks to technology, things that we use everyday in our lives are changing every year. You can now communicate easily with people from almost anywhere in the world thanks to smart phones. Medicine is personalized, and your television set is not a giant box with tubes. The things our children are growing up with did not even exist when we were their ages.

Times are changing, faster and faster. Are you being proactive or reactive to this change?

PLANNING IN REAL TIME – WHY IT WORKS

During the blackout that occurred in the middle of Super Bowl XLVII, Oreo took advantage of the incident to promote their product. "You can still dunk in the dark" became a legendary tweet. This tweet transformed the world of marketing—expanding the concept of instantaneous, real-time marketing.

Using real-time events to post and promote business activities online has quickly become a powerful development in social media marketing. Brands are using current events and occasions that are trending to communicate with consumers – and consumers are responding to them, causing these touches to go viral in record time.

While no one can know exactly what surprises and developments the future holds, you can be ready for them. The key is in planning. Use your imagination to create a vision of where you want to be and then create a plan for how you can get there starting with The One-Page Marketing Plan in the Take Off section. Planning and strategy can make all the difference in growing your company and can make dealing with the future manageable.

YOUR NUMBER ONE

Challenge: Can you simplify your strategy into one thing? What is the number 1 thing you are focused on in your business? (just one)

NUMBER 1:

. . . .

"IF YOU DON'T HAVE A COMPETITIVE ADVANTAGE, DON'T COMPETE." – JACK WELCH

. . . .

SALES	HIRING	ACQUISITION	MESSAGING
PARTNERSHIPS	RETENTION	REPUTATION	GROWTH
CRISIS	EDUCATE	WIN	AUTHENTICITY

AT'S THE NUMBER ONE THING YOU ARE FOCUSED ON? DOES EVERYONE ON THE TEAM KNOW WHAT IT IS AND THEIR ROLE IN ACHIEVING IT?

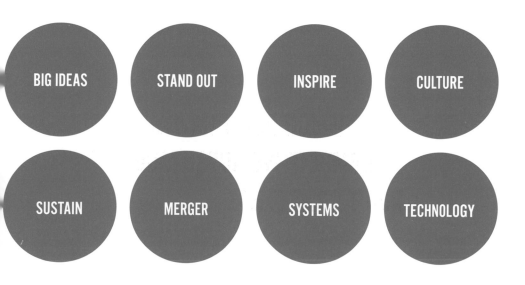

| BIG IDEAS | STAND OUT | INSPIRE | CULTURE |
| SUSTAIN | MERGER | SYSTEMS | TECHNOLOGY |

THE ERA OF THE BRAND

Standing Out has become increasingly challenging in a world of sensory overload. Because of this challenge, a familiar and trusted brand still has the ability to cut through the clutter. Organizations will look deep inside themselves to find those unique characteristics which differentiate them from the competition. Consider these marketing trends when positioning your brand to stand out:

BRAND AWARENESS WILL BE KEY INITIATIVE:
– To stand out, an organization must have a clear idea of where it is standing now.
– Defining key brand attributes (differentiation, relevance, promise and intelligence) will be critical.
– Clarification of core values, mission and vision will lead to authenticity.
– What sets your brand apart will facilitate your distinct advantage.

COMPANY BRAND MUST ALIGN WITH BUSINESS STRATEGY AND PURPOSE:
– Brands have become increasingly disjointed and misunderstood both internally and externally.
– The brand must be consistent with internal and external perceptions, reputation and purpose.
– Alignment will provide a firm foundation on which to build strategy and direction.
– Internal alignment will contribute to team strength and consistent brand and messaging.

BUILDING RELATIONSHIPS IS KEY:

– Intrusive, mass-target marketing is expected to decline as relationships built on trust increase.

– Need to focus on building loyal/long-term relationships rather than quick, short-term acquisitions.

– Nurturing customer relationships will lead to top-of-mind awareness when prospects are ready to buy.

CUSTOMER EXPERIENCE WILL REQUIRE DEDICATED INVESTMENT:

– Customer experience is now at every touch point.

– A primary focus will be technology to improve the customer experience.

– Customers now have abundant choices thanks to search tools, and social networks like Yelp, will make customer experience transparency key in gaining prospects.

– Customer experience will be a top priority for C-Suite.

CUSTOMERS WILL CONTINUE TO VALUE TRANSPARENCY:

– Customers are seeking higher engagement and demanding transparency.

– Brands need to "walk the talk" and create real value for customers.

– If brands do not tell the truth, someone else will do it for them.

– Transparency across all social and digital channels will foster trust and fuel long-term success.

– Genuine messaging will reflect brand alignment.

CONTENT REMAINS KING:
- 86% of B2B organizations are predicted to have content marketing strategies.
- Providing content based on customer wants/needs will build trust and thought leadership.
- Quality content will increase search engine rankings.
- Content co-creation between brands and consumers will continue to rise, creating value to the community where contributors are part of the process.

AUTOMATION IS KEY TO INBOUND MARKETING:
- Inbound strategies continue to be most effective in lead generation and prospect nurturing.
- Compared to 2011, there are 11 times more B2B organizations now using marketing automation.
- Convergence helps businesses stay lean, focused and profitable without compromising quality.
- 97% of B2B marketers will be utilizing an email marketing automation software.
- Content marketing costs 62% less per lead than outbound marketing.

BIG DATA STRATEGIES REMAIN A HIGH PRIORITY:
- Demand will increase for analytical apps like automated reporting, dashboards, predictive measurements and strategic support.
- 68% of organizations use big data to bolster their customer experience and improve process efficiency.
- Big data technology will grow at a 26.4% annual rate through 2018.
- Data will contribute to securing brand and competitor intelligence.

USER EXPERIENCE IS CRUCIAL TO WEBSITE:
- As first point of customer contact, websites must reflect authenticity of the brand.
- Google states the first impression of a webpage happens in the blink of an eye (50 milliseconds to be exact).
- 94% of consumers who rejected or mistrusted a website said it was due to design.
- Website development is now accessible to all levels of users because of the increasing options of pre-made templates.

SOCIAL MEDIA IS THE INTERNET:
- Brands are shifting efforts/budgets from pure SEO to increasing social media optimization.
- 92% of B2B companies use social media in their marketing tactics.
- Search will be extended beyond Google with other channels developing their own search engines, like Facebook.
- Today's consumers are more social in their purchase patterns than ever before.
- 88% of purchasers make choices based on online comments.
- Payment options will increase in usage in social, continuing to grow all-in-one platforms.

VIDEO WILL CONTINUE TO BUILD BRAND EQUITY:
- 74% of all Internet traffic in 2017 will be video.
- 58% of consumers consider companies that produce video content to be more trustworthy, and 71% say that videos leave a positive impression.
- 52% of marketing professionals report video as the mode of content with best ROI.
- Engaging videos boost the chances users will stay on your website longer, increasing SEO.

MOBILE MARKETING IS NOT OPTIONAL:

– Optimizing your website for mobile has become a necessity and a valuable investment.

– Optimizing and making the customer experience easier on a mobile webpage/app increases conversions by 160%.

– 45% of emails are opened on mobile devices.

– Mobile apps will trump traditional ads as advertising and will be used for their functionality.

– Users spend, on average, 82% of their time on mobile with apps and just 18% on browsers.

LOCATION-BASED MARKETING CONTINUES TO RISE:

– Location-based services are expected to bring in $10 billion in revenue (50% will come from location based search advertising).

– Data provides greater precision in targeting, more accurate tracking and insights for optimization.

– Interacting at the right place/time with value, affects purchase decisions and fosters brand advocacy.

ONLINE ADVERTISING WILL SHIFT EVEN MORE TO MOBILE:

– 58% of B2B companies use search engine marketing for paid advertising and only 34% use native advertising.

– Internet ads are expected to grow by 10% globally.

– Mobile ads are expected to grow by 45%.

STORYTELLING = STORYSELLING:
– Visual storytelling will be vital to content marketing success.
– The average human attention span in 2015 is 8.25 seconds.
– Slideshare and other visual presentation programs provide a visual/ interactive way to share.
– With the rising of social live feeds, real-time storytelling will increase.
– Infographics are here to stay to provide complicated information in a visually appealing way.

STANDING OUT IS HOW BRANDS WILL COMPETE:
– The competitive landscape is making it challenging to stand out in the marketplace.
– The New York Times estimated that a person living 30 years ago saw up to 2,000 ad messages a day, compared to over 5,000 seen today.
– To stand out, your brand needs to be more of what makes you who you are.
– Identifying the elements of your distinct advantage and understanding how your brand is perceived will give a clear picture of the opportunities ahead of you.

(Year of the Brand Sources: ContentMarketingInstitute.com, SiriusDecisions "B-to-B Marketing Automation Study," Software Advice and Research Now "Demand Generation Benchmark," HubSpot, 5 IDC.com, Marketing and Management Sciences Book, Bright Local Consumer Review Survey, Google's Brand Lab, Animoto.com Survey (featured in NY Times, CNN, NBC, Bloomberg), EMarketer, NetElixir.com, Adestra Report On Top 10 Email Clients, Harvard Business Review, InboundNow. com, Huffington Post)

MARKETING TRENDS

PRIMARY TREND TO FOCUS ON:

MARKETING TRENDS:

- [ ] Brand Awareness
- [ ] Strategy Alignment
- [ ] Relationships
- [ ] Customer Experience
- [ ] Transparency
- [ ] Content
- [ ] Marketing Automation

- [ ] Big Data
- [ ] Online Experience
- [ ] Social Marketing
- [ ] Video
- [ ] Mobilization
- [ ] Location Marketing
- [ ] Online Advertising
- [ ] Storyselling

OTHER:

Marketing Trend Exercise: Which marketing trends influence the future success of your brand?

BUSINESS / BRAND STRATEGY ALIGNMENT

BUSINESS STRATEGY:

BRAND STRATEGY:

HOW THE BUSINESS STRATEGY
SUPPORTS THE BRAND:

HOW THE BRAND STRATEGY
SUPPORTS THE BUSINESS:

ALIGNED GOAL:

Brand / Strategy Alignment: The goal is alignment. Start with the aligned goal, then explore independent strategies that complement and support each.

FOCUS AND DISCIPLINE MAY WORK ON PAPER, BUT IT GETS HARDER WHEN YOU BEGIN TO IMPLEMENT AND ARE CONTINUOUSLY DISTRACTED.

THERE IS FOCUS AND COMMITMENT TO ACHIEVE DESIRED RESULTS.

· ·

MINDSET

· ·

IDENTIFY WHERE YOU STAND.

Which of these statements most accurately reflects the focus and commitment to achieve the desired results?

- [ ] We do not have a disciplined mindset.
- [ ] We somewhat have a disciplined mindset.
- [ ] We have a disciplined mindset, but as a team, we are not all committed to achieving desired results.
- [ ] We have a disciplined mindset, we are committed to achieving desired results, but we are not focused.
- [ ] We have a disciplined mindset, we are focused and we are committed to achieving desired results.

THROUGHOUT EACH WORKDAY, WE AIM TO ACHIEVE RESULTS. THE MORE WE HAVE TO DEAL WITH, THE MORE OUR ABILITY TO FOCUS IS CHALLENGED. WITH DISTRACTIONS INCREASINGLY BECOMING A PART OF EACH DAY, EVEN THE MOST DISCIPLINED PERSON CAN LOSE CONCENTRATION AND BE SIDE-TRACKED. HOW CAN WE STAY FOCUSED ON WHAT NEEDS TO BE DONE TO ACHIEVE THE GOALS WE SET?

Here are a few simple steps that work:

Set goals. Setting goals that are specific, measurable, achievable, realistic and timely will help you commit to achieving your desired results. Setting up goals will help you discipline yourself in order to see outcomes.

Hold yourself accountable. Sometimes when we don't receive desired results it is because we make excuses. We don't "feel like it." Not allowing excuses is the first step in accountability. Holding yourself to a higher standard will help you reach the goals you set for yourself.

Remove distractions. Distractions are one of the biggest reasons we lose focus. Without focused attention, discipline is impossible. Removing those things that will distract you from reaching your results will help discipline your mentality.

A disciplined mindset is essential. But like anything else, practice makes perfect. Don't expect to become a disciplined mastermind within a day. Make lists, set reminders, and do whatever you need to do to keep yourself in focus and accomplish the outcomes you want.

FOCUS AND EMPLOYEES

With today's modern technology, the workplace is becoming increasingly distracting. On average, people check their phones 150 times per day. With most work being done on computers, workers may have access to the Internet all day long. Distraction can be just one click away. So how do you get employees to focus?

Hold Them Accountable. Give your employees responsibilities and hold them to those tasks. Employees can also hold each other accountable through teamwork. Maintaining a strong team environment can help focus employees because they know others are depending on them.

Show Them the Big Picture. Explain to employees the part their jobs play in the big picture. Let them know how their duties fit into the rest of the organization. Employees are more likely to focus and have a disciplined mindset when they know that their work is affecting the entire organization.

Mindset (Measurement). Even the best marketing strategy is incomplete without measurements. Metrics matter because they let you know if your actions and efforts are producing positive results—if you're advancing toward your goals. Without metrics, how would you know for sure?

Set Goals. Before measurement can begin, it's important to determine exactly what you want to measure. Set specific goals—and really get specific—don't just set a goal of more leads, make it specific: ten new leads per week is specific.

WHAT DO YOU WANT TO ACCOMPLISH THROUGH YOUR MARKETING EFFORTS?

What types of media will you use to communicate? Do you want to drive traffic to your website or do you want emails or phone calls? With your goal in mind, select a new strategy or adjust your current one accordingly, and then set a reasonable deadline.

Use Available Tools. Research the different tools available that you can use to measure social media data. You may also notice the many companies that provide services for this. After research, pick the tools or services that will be most beneficial for you and your business. You may already have access to some, like Facebook Analytics.

Watch On Your Own. While your networks are being measured, you can still play a part. Observe and monitor your business's Facebook, Twitter, and other profiles. How does your audience appear to be responding to your messages? If you notice any problems, fix the issues and respond to the audience. Your awareness and attention may affect the measurements (in a good way!) in the long run.

Learn From Your Results. Your measurements should allow you to compare your results, to view your performance over time and to notice trends for what works and what doesn't work. Use this information to make adjustments to your strategy. Remember that online and social media are subjective and still growing, so there's no one definitive tool that will work for everyone in the same way. Your measurements should assist in tracking the progress you've made, so that you can continue getting the best results from your marketing strategy.

MEASURING SUCCESS

Twins are always competing between themselves. With so much in common, they have to find ways to outdo each other. One of the "competitions" between my identical twin sister Lorrie and I was pretty simple—who was the tallest? In the house we grew up in, we had a measuring tape on the inside of our bedroom door. Every so often, our parents would have us stand with our backs to the measuring tape, marking where the tops of our heads reached with a black marker. I'm sure every child has been measured like this at some point, but I had the pressure of being measured next to my twin. Lorrie was always just a little bit taller than me.

I desperately wanted to be taller, to win this "competition." I tried to stand as straight as I could during the measurements, but Lorrie always won—only by a little, but it was enough. I never quite caught up to her, but in the years since, I've learned that there are other ways to measure success.

In business, we often try to measure our success, which can be a pretty metaphorical process. Using analytics as a resource helps you measure your business's success in a more concrete way. Consider the goals that you set when you started using social media for your business. Are you accomplishing what you wanted to, like driving more traffic to your website or building brand awareness? Metrics can help you see that answer more clearly.

The number of "likes" or "retweets" that you get doesn't really tell you if your overall strategy is working—it's not an accurate measure of the success of your campaign. When you use specific tools for measurement, though, you will be presented with much more relevant information about the results of your campaign. Different metrics tools will give you different information, like demographics on people who have liked your content, how many people looked at your page, or trends that demonstrate which strategies are working, and which aren't. With this information, you can decide how to make adjustments to your social marketing strategy.

In business, we need to use analytics to measure our campaigns' success. These metrics help us know when we need to make changes, and changes keep us growing.

CREATING A DASHBOARD

Picture the dashboard in your car. You've probably glanced at it so many times that you have the layout memorized. Everything that you need to know when you're driving is right there, from your speed, to your mileage, to the level of gas in your tank, to the "check engine" light that alerts you of a potential problem. You rely on the information your dashboard provides at a glance to keep you driving safely.

Dashboards are equally important online tools that can support your marketing. These dashboards are organizational in nature. When you look at your marketing dashboard, you should see visual representations of your marketing campaigns. Dashboards can be customized to display what you think is most important or relevant to your efforts and your plan.

It's important that your dashboards are easy to understand. Whether their purpose is to condense a wealth of information into understandable graphics or charts, or to keep information easily accessible with less clutter, your dashboards should be clear and comprehensive. They exist for your own benefit, and since you typically get to choose what widgets or windows you see, you need to have them relatively organized. A dashboard can't help you much if you can't follow or understand it!

Ultimately, your dashboard should help you increase productivity. Once dashboards have been set up to your liking, they should be a help, not a hindrance. Learning to navigate them may take time, but it will be well worth the effort. Following your trends, patterns, and metrics can tell you how to adjust your marketing strategy, while making multiple updates to multiple networks through one tool can save you time and stress.

All dashboards are different. No two services provide exactly the same dashboard options or layouts. To get the full benefits that dashboards can provide, you need to select the ones that are the easiest for you to understand—the ones that make the most sense for your strategy. Research the different dashboard services to decide which one suits your needs.

FOCUS.

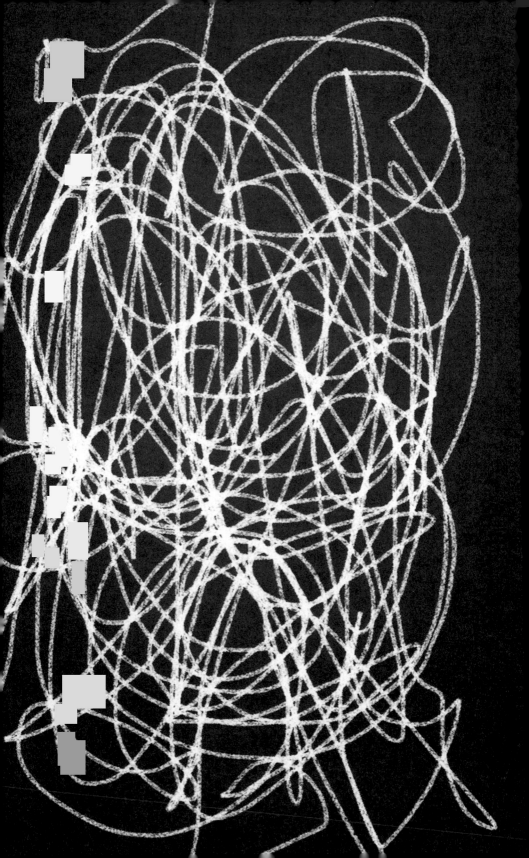

WHAT'S ON YOUR DASHBOARD?

Opportunities:

- [ ] New Leads
- [ ] Marketing Qualified Leads
- [ ] Sales Qualified Leads
- [ ] Off Radar

Sales:

- [ ] Calls
- [ ] Proposals
- [ ] Closed Sales

Campaigns:

- [ ] Weekly Goal
- [ ] Monthly Results

Team:

- [ ] Wing Earners
- [ ] Daily Huddle
- [ ] Weekly Team Meeting
- [ ] Quarterly Event

Planning:

- [ ] Monthly
- [ ] Quarterly
- [ ] Annual Summit

Awareness:

- [ ] Website Visits
- [ ] Social Following

Engagement:

- [ ] Social Media Interactions
- [ ] E-mail
- [ ] Offer Conversions

....

Dashboard: What's on your dashboard? What should be? Keep it simple—what metrics do you need to review on a daily, weekly, monthly and annual basis to stay on course?

....

MINDSET

START:

STOP:

CONTINUE:

Mindset Exercise: What would be beneficial to start doing? What two things are you doing that are not working or are ineffective? What two things are you currently doing that are effective?

SO MANY TIMES WE CREATE A BIG IDEA,
THEN WE GET STUCK ON THE RUNWAY BECAUSE WE ARE NOT CLEAR ON
WHICH DIRECTION TO TAKE OFF.

☐ THE ONE-PAGE MARKETING PLAN™
☐ OFF THE RADAR

TAKE OFF

YOU HAVE ASSESSED THE STRENGTHS AND WEAKNESSES OF YOUR BRAND. YOU HAVE ESTABLISHED THE PURPOSE OF YOUR COMPANY. YOU HAVE ASSESSED INTERNAL AND EXTERNAL PERCEPTIONS AND THOSE THAT NEED TO BE CHANGED. YOU HAVE DETERMINED THE DISTINCT ADVANTAGES THAT DIFFERENTIATE YOU FROM YOUR COMPETITORS AND YOU KNOW WHO YOUR IDEAL CLIENTS ARE.

IT'S TIME TO TAKE OFF.

THIS IS WHEN YOU DETERMINE NOT ONLY WHAT IT IS THAT YOU WANT TO STAND OUT FOR BUT HOW YOU WILL MAKE THIS HAPPEN. IT'S CRITICAL THAT YOU ESTABLISH AND CONTROL HOW YOUR BUSINESS BECOMES DISTINGUISHED IN THE MARKETPLACE. YOU HAVE DONE THAT. WHAT YOU NEED NOW IS A PLAN OF ACTION. THIS HIGH LEVEL ONE-PAGE MARKETING PLAN™ GUIDES YOU TO:

- ☐ Increasing exposure of your company's authentic personality.
- ☐ Uncovering big sky ideas.
- ☐ Building stronger relationships internally and externally.
- ☐ Communicating your company's unique qualities and differentiators.
- ☐ Aligning internal and external messaging.
- ☐ Focusing your strategy to key activities that lead to specific results.
- ☐ Targeting and nurturing your ideal leads.
- ☐ Building a high level plan that can be measured.

THE ONE-PAGE MARKETING PLAN™

Components include:

- ☐ Organizational Purpose
- ☐ Distinct Advantage
- ☐ Brand Positioning
- ☐ Brand Persona
- ☐ What Do You Stand For
- ☐ Brand Traffic Radar
- ☐ Ideal Lead
- ☐ Big Sky Idea
- ☐ Lead Strategy
- ☐ Key Messaging
- ☐ Off Radar Opportunities
- ☐ Key Campaigns
- ☐ Take Off Campaign
- ☐ Key Issues
- ☐ Top 5
- ☐ Number 1
- ☐ Wing Earners
- ☐ Quarterly Targets

One-Page Marketing Plan™: Go to www.TwinEngine.com/BTC to download the One-Page Marketing Plan™. If you need help building your plan contact StandOut@TwinEngine.com.

Preparation:

☐ **Read the book** *Stand Out:* To order copies, go to www.TwinEngine.com/StandOut or Amazon.com.

☐ **Take the Brand Traffic Control Assessment**: go to www. TwinEngine.com/BTC to assess what areas of The 8 Fundamentals you need to strengthen.

☐ **Brand Intelligence:** Review online intelligence relative to your brand, business, key employees and industry.

☐ **Competitive Intelligence:** Review online intelligence of the competition.

☐ **Schedule a planning meeting.**

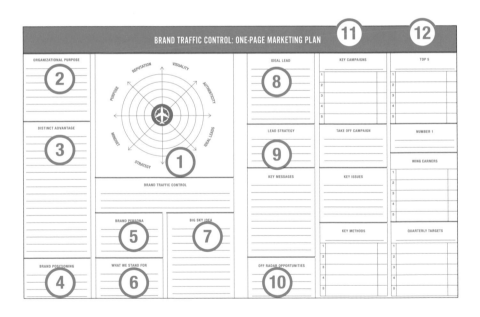

• •

One-Page Marketing Plan™: Each activity is numbered with brief instructions. If you have questions and/or need help building your plan contact StandOut@TwinEngine.com

• •

1. BRAND TRAFFIC CONTROL™ RADAR

The Brand Traffic Control Radar is designed to assess the strength and alignment of your brand on 8 Fundamentals of Standing out in business: Purpose, Reputation, Visuality, Authenticity, Ideal Leads, Distinction, Strategy and Mindset.

Action:

☐ Refer to the introduction or go to www.TwinEngine.com/BTC to download the radar to plot your opinion of the current position of your organization within each indicator on a scale of zero in the center (non-existent) to five on the outside ring (highest level).

Checklist:

☐ What areas need strengthening?

☐ Are the individual team scores aligned on each of the fundamentals?

. . . .

Notes:

2. ORGANIZATIONAL PURPOSE

Answer the questions below and you can gain a clearer idea of what your purpose is and how it fits into what your business does.

What do you love? What activities do you most enjoy?

What does the world need? What do you do that adds value to the world?

What do you do really well? What are your talents and skills?

What would the world pay for it? What do you do that others value and want, and how much do they want it?

Action:

☐ Refer to the activities in the section on Purpose to engage your team to discuss each of the aspects that lead to discovering your organization's purpose. Break into small groups and share outcomes.

Checklist:

☐ Our purpose is clear.

☐ We know what we stand for.

☐ Our purpose is consistently communicated.

. . . .

Notes:

3. DISTINCT ADVANTAGE

Your distinct advantage is not just what makes your product or service different, it's what makes your company different — and what your company stands for and why it's in business. It is the unique combination of gifts, experiences, culture, stories, skills and inclinations that make up who you are and what you do in ways that your competition doesn't, can't and won't.

Action:

☐ Refer to the activities in the section on Distinction to engage your team to discuss what your ideal clients want that you provide that your competitors don't. Use findings to identify your distinct advantages.

Checklist:

☐ We stand out from our competitors.

☐ We stand out to our influencers.

☐ We stand out among industry thought leaders.

. . . .

Notes:

4. BRAND POSITIONING

Like a GPS directional device, our Brand Positioning Assessment shows you where you are relative to where you want to go.

Brand Differentiation – How effectively does your brand capture the attention of prospects?

Brand Relevance – How aligned is your brand to your customers' and prospects' needs?

Brand Promise – How consistently does your brand deliver on its promises?

Brand Intelligence – How well does your company understand its brand and the quality and impact of the brand experience on your customers?

Action:
- ☐ To download this assessment to evaluate the current position of your brand go to www.TwinEngine.com/BTC.

Checklist:
- ☐ Our brand is properly positioned.
- ☐ We understand what differentiates our brand .
- ☐ We leverage our brand equity.

. . . .

Notes:

5. BRAND PERSONA

When your story, messages and images reflect the values, personality, and lifestyle preferences of your audience, they'll feel more involved with your brand. And ultimately your product or service becomes an obvious choice as an extension of your story. The key is authenticity—aligning what you communicate about your company, products or services with whom you truly are. If the personality a company attempts to portray is just a façade, a mask for what it truly is, then its storytelling attempts to create an appealing personality will eventually fail.

Action:

☐ Refer to the activities in the sections on Visuality and Authenticity to explore what words, images and personality traits create your brand persona.

Checklist:

☐ Who we are on the outside is aligned with who we are on the inside

· ·

Notes:

6. WHAT WE STAND FOR

Now more than ever, your company's success is determined by how clearly you define and communicate your core values and qualities. In short, it's all about what you stand for. What do you stand for? Whether your business is established or new, you have to know what you stand for before your customers can know. Do you know?

The question has become not only how can you stand out, but what will you stand for? It's crucial that you direct how your business distinguishes itself in the marketplace.

Action:

☐ Refer to the activities in the section on Authenticity to explore how you communicate what you stand for to the world.

Checklist:

☐ We know what we stand for.

☐ What we stand for is consistently communicated.

· ·

Notes:

7. BIG SKY IDEA

What out-of-the box ideas can you launch that will take your brand and company to big sky success? All companies compete with other companies. How can you get above the clouds to compete in blue skies and stand out from everyone else?

Action:

☐ Look for opportunities to improve your products and services. Refer to the Big Sky Idea activity in the section on Purpose. Poll your team and ask these questions: What is the next idea that is going to take you to the next level? What big idea is going to help you stand out?

Checklist:

☐ We think bigger and out-of-the-box when it comes to blue skies.

☐ We have a big idea that's going to take us to the next level.

· ·

Notes:

8. IDEAL LEAD

The first step to creating an ideal lead flow is to agree on a set of criteria about what an ideal lead looks like, then develop a profile to better focus your sales and marketing team's efforts. The following are examples of information that you may include in your lead profile:

☐ A set of demographics that includes job level and seniority.

☐ A day in their life.

☐ A list of their pain points, motivations and goals.

☐ Where do they look for information?

Action:

☐ Refer to the activities in the section on Ideal Leads. Profile your ideal lead to understand their role, motivations and the challenges they face professionally and personally.

Checklist:

☐ We know the persona of our ideal lead.

☐ We have identified profiles for each of our target audiences.

☐ We know the behaviors of our ideal leads.

· ·

Notes:

9. KEY MESSAGES

When an organization's words match who it is and what it believes and its actions match its words, it is being authentic. Start with the question: "Who are you?" Your company is made up of layers. To truly be authentic, you must examine each of these layers until you reach the core of your beliefs, vision and goals. This is where you find who you are and what you represent as a company.

From there, every business action and decision you make should reflect who you are. Your authentic self is a collection of all of the things that make you and your business unique and individual—your passions, talents, inclinations, life experiences and especially your values and beliefs—what you stand for and why you're in the business you're in.

Action:

☐ Refer to the section on Authenticity to explore what words, images and personality traits create your brand persona.

Checklist:

☐ Our messages are authentic and true.

☐ We know what people say about our brand.

· ·

Notes:

10. OFF RADAR OPPORTUNITIES

What's missing in your industry? Differentiation can come from filling a space in your industry that doesn't exist. What opportunities exist that may be outside your radar? Is there something missing that will take your organization to the next level to explore unchartered opporunities?

Actions:

- ☐ Poll your team, ask your customers. Refer to the activities in the section on Reputation.
- ☐ Look everywhere – your products and services, the competition, other industries...
- ☐ What problems in your industry need solutions that you could provide?
- ☐ What frustrates you, your clients and your industry the most that could lead to new solutions?

Checklist:

- ☐ We have identified Off Radar Opportunities.
- ☐ We discuss Off Radar Opportunities at every strategic planning session.

· ·

Notes:

11/12. GOALS AND MEASUREMENT

Key Campaigns:

☐ What are the top 5 campaigns that align with your marketing strategy?

Take Off Campaign:

☐ How are you going to launch your Big Sky Idea to your internal team, employees and partners?

Key Issues:

☐ What are the key issues your industry faces and how do those issues impact your planned campaigns?

Key Methods:

☐ What are the key methods by which you will deliver your marketing strategy?

Top 5:

☐ What are the Top 5 initiatives that are going to help your organization Stand Out?

Number 1:

☐ What is the number 1 thing (just one) that will be the focus each quarter?

Wing Earners:

☐ What milestones/goals will you celebrate?

Quarterly Targets:

☐ What are your top 5 quarterly targets?

OFF THE RADAR

WHAT IS MISSING IN YOUR INDUSTRY:

WHAT PROBLEM NEEDS TO BE SOLVED?

WHAT DOES THE FUTURE LOOK LIKE:

Off the Radar Exercise: Bring together a diverse team to explore ideas, then rate each idea on impact and potential for success.

ONE-PAGE MARKETING PLAN™ FOCUS

NUMBER 1 AREA OF FOCUS:

OFF THE RADAR OPPORTUNITIES THAT SUPPORT THE AREA OF FOCUS:

NEXT STEPS/OWNER:

One-Page Marketing Plan Focus Exercise: What is your number 1 area of focus? How do your off the radar opportunities support it? What are the next steps and who is responsible for each?

YOUR GOAL IS NOT JUST OUT IN THE FUTURE; THE DAILY GOAL IS STAYING ON COURSE, STEADILY BUILDING YOUR BRAND AND BUILDING BRAND EQUITY AS WELL.

☐ **BRAND TRAFFIC CONTROL CHECKLIST**

· ·

ON COURSE

· ·

STAYING ON COURSE IS A DYNAMIC AND CON-
TINUAL PROCESS. OVER THE COURSE OF YOUR
BUSINESS LIFE ANY ONE OR ALL OF THE 8 FUN-
DAMENTALS COULD CHANGE AT ONE TIME OR
ANOTHER AND FOR A VARIETY OF REASONS. WE
ENCOURAGE YOU TO MAKE REVISITING THE PRO-
CESSES WE HAVE OUTLINED IN THIS BOOK PART
OF YOUR ANNUAL EVALUATION, STRATEGY AND
PLANNING.

To download a PDF go to www.TwinEngine.com/BTC to access the
Brand Traffic Control checklist.

THE 90% RULE. BEFORE A PILOT TAKES OFF ON A FLIGHT, HE CREATES A FLIGHT PLAN. HE KNOWS HIS DESTINATION AND APPROXIMATELY HOW LONG IT WILL TAKE TO GET THERE. HE LIFTS OFF AT THE SCHEDULED TIME, BUT DURING THE COURSE OF THE FLIGHT AIR TURBULENCE, WEATHER CONDITIONS, AND OTHER FACTORS KEEP PUSHING THE PLANE OFF COURSE. IN FACT, THE PLANE IS OFF COURSE ABOUT 90 PERCENT OF THE TIME. 90%! *(Source: Stephen R. Covey, How to Develop Your Personal Mission Statement)*

So, how does the pilot get to his final destination on schedule? By making constant course corrections throughout the flight. He gathers information regularly from his instruments, from radar and weather reports and from ground control technicians along the way. Using this data he evaluates his current location relative to his destination and makes adjustments to get back on course.

Starting and running a business is a lot like a pilot preparing to take off. You have a specific destination. You create a business 'flight' plan, assemble the resources you need and begin your journey. But as your company has grown, it's possible that the picture you envisioned as your destination has become less clear, overshadowed by the day-to-day details of business. You are off course. And without course corrections, you might not reach your desired destination.

STAYING ON COURSE

Alignment is the unifying thread running through and connecting all of The 8 Fundamentals. It is the overarching goal of Staying on Course and a dynamic situation for any business. The fundamentals are a system; a bit like a mobile. They work together and, under optimum conditions, they support one another. But when one is deficient and out of balance, it affects the others. Likewise, an improvement in one that is deficient can make a significant difference in the others. The overall affect of focusing on alignment of the fundamentals is that it improves a company's performance better and more efficiently than by focusing on any one fundamental alone.

Examples of brands that continue to stay on course:

UPS–Founded in 1907 to fill the need for private messenger and delivery services, UPS's history reflects a continual focus on keeping up with industry changes, innovations and technologies while staying connected to their core common carrier service, including daily pickup calls, payment to the shipper, additional delivery attempts, streamlined documentation and comparable rates – which have been part of their service since 1922. Pioneering use of the automobile, conveyor belt systems and airplanes have all contributed to their success, still today, as the world's largest package delivery company and a provider of supply chain management solutions.

John Deere–It started in 1837 with a hardworking blacksmith who developed the first commercially successful, self-scouring steel plow. The company was then and remains committed to the success of those linked to the land. Having farmers for clients can present financial challenges, but this company believes that from challenges come opportunities. While living up to a legacy isn't always easy, the company attributes its success to having strong, decisive leaders at its helm, dedicated to the core principles of integrity, quality, commitment and innovation.

Google–Founded in 1998 to organize the world's information and make it universally accessible and useful, Google has become the guru of online search. Their frequent algorithms keep us all on our toes, and do more to contribute to keeping the Internet fresh than probably any other single thing. They have given a whole new meaning to the words "computer geek." While they maintain the culture of a start-up, they now employ 40,000+ people in 70 offices in 40 countries. They are smart, curious, creative and cohesive. There are Ten Things they know to be true which they have followed from the start and which may be their secret to staying on course.

BRAND TRAFFIC CONTROL CHECKLIST

Staying on course requires regular and consistent monitoring of the fundamentals that are integral to a company continuing to Stand Out. This checklist is designed to assist in interim evaluations. Statements define levels of accomplishment required to be on course. Unchecked boxes indicate areas needing improvement.

1. PURPOSE: The organization knows and lives its purpose; it knows what it stands for and is true to its beliefs

- [ ] **Purpose** = Our purpose is clear, we know what we stand for, and it is consistently communicated.

- [ ] **What We Stand For** = We know what we stand for and it is consistently communicated internally and externally.

- [ ] **Stories** = Stories that support the purpose of the organization are documented and shared.

2. REPUTATION: The organization monitors brand perception, industry trends and the competitive landscape

- [ ] **Key Issues** = Organization stays updated on the key issues that its industry faces.

- [ ] **Brand Chatter** = Organization monitors what is being said about its brand, products and team members weekly.

- [ ] **Industry Chatter** = Organization monitors leading industry topics and trends weekly.

- [ ] **Competitive Monitoring** = Organization monitors what is being said about key competitors.

3. VISUALITY: The outward appearance of the brand truly reflects who the organization is and the value it delivers

☐ **First Impression** = The outward appearance of the brand truly reflects who the organization is and the value it delivers.

☐ **Consistency** = The brand is presented consistently on all channels internally and externally.

☐ **Brand Survey** = The brand is surveyed annually (internally and externally) to assess its strengths and weaknesses.

☐ **Monitoring** = The organization monitors how the brand is expressed externally and has a response plan in place.

4. AUTHENTICITY: The organization's messaging is consistent, true, genuine and communicates value propositions

☐ **Key Messages** = The key messages of the organization are defined, shared and continuously updated.

☐ **Authenticity** = The key messages of the organization are genuine.

☐ **Value Propositions** = The organization has defined and shares primary and secondary value propositions.

☐ **Voice** = The brand voice is defined and consistent in all communications.

☐ **Elevator Speech** = Each team member can consistently respond to the question 'What do you do?'.

5. LEADS: Consistent funnel of ideal leads is nurtured and managed

☐ **Lead Strategy** = A strategy is defined to nurture and manage leads

☐ **Preferred Passengers** = Team members can identify ideal leads and know profiles, motivations and behaviors.

☐ **Brand Persona** = The brand persona addresses the demographics, psychographics and motivations of ideal leads.

☐ **Stowaways** = The team knows how to identify high maintenance / low revenue leads/clients.

6. DISTINCTION: Stands out among its competitors, influencers and industry thought leaders

☐ **Big Sky Idea** = Organization has defined the big idea that sets it apart from the competition.

☐ **Protected Air Space** = The team has identified the areas in the market in which it has significant advantages.

☐ **Distinct Advantage** = The distinct advantage that separates from the competition is defined.

☐ **Take Off Campaign** = Organization develops and launches an annual internal 'Take Off' theme and campaign.

7. STRATEGY: A 12-month marketing strategy is in force and aligned with the organization's goals

☐ **Marketing Plan** = A 12-month marketing plan is in place and updated quarterly.

☐ **Alignment** = The marketing plan is in alignment with the strategic business plan and core initiatives.

☐ **Annual Planning** = An annual meeting identifies business and marketing initiatives for the year.

☐ **Brand Equity** = The methods to deliver the brand are leveraged.

☐ **Editorial Calendar** = Organization maintains a monthly messaging strategy and editorial calendar.

8. MINDSET: Focus and commitment to achieve desired results

☐ **Number 1** = The number 1 priority is defined and updated quarterly.

☐ **Disciplined Mindset** = The team is focused and has a disciplined mindset.

☐ **Top 5** = The team identifies the top 5 marketing initiatives and monitors monthly.

☐ **Brand Standards** = The brand is clearly defined and the brand standards portfolio is up to date.

☐ **Off The Radar** = The team meets quarterly to explore unchartered areas for exploration and growth.

BRAND TRAFFIC CONTROL CHECKLIST

NUMBER 1 FUNDAMENTAL THAT NEEDS STRENGTHENING:

TOP 5 AREAS THAT NEED IMPROVEMENT:

Brand Traffic Control Checklist Summary: What is the number 1 fundamental that needs strengthening? What are the top 5 areas that need improvement?

FIRST THINGS FIRST: **STAND OUT** IS MORE THAN

A STATEMENT – **IT'S A CHALLENGE.**

READY?

NOW THAT YOU HAVE KNOWLEDGE OF THE FUNDAMENTALS OF WHAT IT TAKES TO STAND OUT AND THE SPECIFIC TOOLS TO TAKE YOU TO THE NEXT STEP, WILL YOU TAKE IT?

WILL YOU MAKE THE EFFORT TO DEFINE YOUR PURPOSE? TO DIFFERENTIATE YOURSELF BY IDENTIFYING YOUR DISTINCT ADVANTAGE? WILL YOU TAKE THE STEPS TO ALIGN WHO YOU ARE WITH WHAT YOU DO AND USE THE POWER OF YOUR AUTHENTICITY TO DISTINGUISH YOURSELF FROM THE COMPETITION? LOOKING AT WHERE YOU ARE NOW, DOES IT ALL SEEM OVERWHELMING? OR, HAVE YOU ALREADY DONE THE WORK NEEDED TO ALIGN YOUR EFFORTS INTERNALLY TO GET THE MOST FROM YOUR ORGANIZATION AND PEOPLE.

We wrote this book to help business leaders gain a unique perspective on how their businesses can stand out. It's meant to introduce tools and resources to help a business define who it is (distinct advantage), clarify how it represents itself to its prospects and customers (brand) and align these in practical ways to achieve specific measurable goals (strategy).

The concepts and exercises are specifically structured to uncover what is missing from your business plan or marketing strategy. They are also designed to help you become more of who you already are, and inspire you to become the success you were destined to be. It can be overwhelming to try to keep track of how and if your brand is being noticed and preferred by prospects and customers. How can you know with any certainty if your brand is on course or lost among dozens or even thousands of competitive brands?

Brand Traffic Control is designed to provide organizations with a new way of aligning their brands. Using straightforward tools, it shows how to strengthen and master The 8 Fundamentals of Standing Out in Business. When you strengthen them, your brand will stand out; you'll know where you are relative to your competition; you'll know how to create consistent messaging to your ideal lead to increase engagement; your brand will be in alignment; you'll be able to execute plans more effectively; you'll know what makes your brand distinct; you'll have a tool to measure what's working and what isn't; and, you'll be able to position your brand to take off.

Turn to the next page for the top 5 things you can do to start standing out today!

5 THINGS TO DO TO START STANDING OUT

Thank you for reading our book! If you need support or a facilitator to lead your strategic plan implementation, we're here to help - StandOut@TwinEngine.com.

Here are the 5 things you can do now to start standing out, today!

1. READ AND SHARE THE BOOK:
- [ ] **Download the executive summary** – www.TwinEngine.com/BTC.
- [ ] **Share the book with your team** – Collaborate on areas of focus.
- [ ] **Top 10 take-aways** – Identify your top 10 take-aways and next steps.

2. TAKE THE ASSESSMENT:
- [ ] **Take the Assessment** – www.TwinEngine.com/BTC.
- [ ] **The Eight Fundamentals** – Know where you stand and what fundamentals need strengthening.

3. ALIGN YOUR BUSINESS STRATEGY AND BRAND STRATEGY:
- [ ] **Read the section on Strategy.**
- [ ] **Brand / Strategy Alignment Exercise** – Refer to the exercises in the Strategy section.
- [ ] **Get Aligned** – Start with the aligned goal, then explore independent strategies that complement and support each.

4. DISCOVER YOUR DISTINCT ADVANTAGE:
- [ ] **Read the section on Distinction.**
- [ ] **Discover Your Distinct Advantage** – Refer to the exercises in the Distinction section.

5. PLAN YOUR STRATEGY SUMMIT:
- [ ] **Read the sections on Strategy and Take Off.**
- [ ] **Set a Date** – Plan a full day team summit.
- [ ] **Complete The One-Page Marketing Plan™** – Refer to The One-Page Marketing Plan instructions in the Take Off section.

SOME OF OUR FAVORITE **STAND OUT** RESOURCES

STAND OUT RESOURCES

PURPOSE:

How to Fascinate:

This resource helps identify either your personal or brand's highest value and help communicate it externally. With these tools, you can discover a new way to measure how the world sees you or your brand.

www.howtofascinate.com

Know your WHY:

When you know your WHY you realize your unique gift and you live with passion. You know why you do what you do, how you think, what you believe – your purpose in life. And when your business expresses and lives its WHY, you build a winning team with clarity, vision and a unified culture – becoming an inspired business.

www.KnowYourWHY.com

Start with Why:

Do you know your Why? The purpose, cause, or belief that inspires you to do what you do? Simon Sinek's online Why Discovery Course can help you learn and live your Why.

www.StartWithWhy.com

REPUTATION:

Google Alerts:

This notification database alerts you to any new results — web pages, newspaper articles, blogs, videos — that match your search term. With this resource, you can monitor — in real time — what is being said about your brand, your competition and/or your industry based on key terms that are used.

www.google.com/alerts

Meltwater:

This tool allows you to listen to conversations, understand your impact on the market, engage with key influencers and measure your performance against competitors. With this resource, you access news, trends and practices in traditional and social media intelligence.

www.meltwater.com

Radian6:

This tool allows you to watch, analyze and engage with information that is being shared online. With this resource, you can actively monitor any brand mentions across all social media channels and create reports to measure performance.

www.salesforce.com/radian6

Social Mention:

This social media search engine allows you to monitor what is being said about your brand, your competitors, your industry or any topic across all social channels in real-time. With this tool, you can combine all online user generated content based on trends, topics and keywords into a single medium to perform analyses.

www.socialmention.com

Trackur:

This resource offers social media measurement tools and analytics to help you monitor the reputation of your brand. With this tool, you are able to access data to monitor social results and see who is talking about your company, your brand and your products.

www.trackur.com

AUTHENTICITY:

Media Shower:

This content marketing solution provides your business with content that grows your business by attracting traffic, leads and customers. With this resource, you are not only given access to unique content, but content promotions as well.

www.mediashower.com

TextBroker:

This content writing service allows you to buy unique content for your company to capture your audience's attention. Writers with a variety of industry experience can assist in capturing your brand's voice.

www.textbroker.com

Writers Access:

This resource allows you to hire freelance writers to provide content for your brand marketing. With this platform, you can find a suitable writer to express your voice, place orders and manage workflow.

www.writeraccess.com

IDEAL LEADS:

HubSpot:

This easy to use inbound marketing software platform helps companies attract visitors, convert leads, and close customers. It includes all the tools you need to master inbound marketing - creating content, SEO, social media, landing pages, calls to actions, personalized email and website.

www.hubspot.com

Square 2 Marketing:

This inbound marketing agency generates leads and drives revenue for your business through web design and inbound marketing strategies. With this HubSpot Diamond Partner, every strategy and tactic is specialized for your business in order to help you stand out from the competition.

www.square2marketing.com

STRATEGY:

The Awesome Institute:

Awesome Institute helps entrepreneurs live satisfying lives while running great businesses. Through short, dynamic, online classes, coaching, and workshops, the real life of entrepreneurship is explored and ways to deal with the stress, frustration and loneliness, allowing you to design and actually move towards a life and business that you truly love.

www.awesomeinstitute.com

EOS: Entrepreneur Operating System:

This system is a complete set of concepts and practical tools that help entrepreneurs get what they want from their businesses by focusing on 3 major areas: vision, traction, and health. Training and support are offered to effectively implement this system into your business.

www.eosworldwide.com

Entrepreneurs' Organization:

Entrepreneurs' Organization is an exclusive network of entrepreneurs focused on business, personal development and community. This network allows entrepreneurs to learn from each other in order to succeed in business and personal life goals.

www.eonetwork.org

Gazelles:

This resource gives you access to strategic intelligence to help your business reach its potential. With tools for strategic planning, a strategic program and a book about mastering strategy within your business, this resource sets your company up for long term success.

www.gazelles.com

Jack Daly:

This resource offers keynote presentations, workshops, seminars and training sessions to inspire you to take action in the areas of sales, sales management, customer loyalty and motivation. Jack provides the tools and knowledge to successfully sell in today's business environment.

www.jackdaly.com

Petra Coach:

This business consulting service helps a business define priorities, implement a system to ensure the priorities are met and build a culture of alignment, accountability and purpose. This coaching program ensures accountability within your organization and your team in order to get things done.

www.petracoach.com

MINDSET:

Dandapani:

Dandapani is a renowned speaker who shares his unique techniques with top business leaders and entrepreneurs in order to unlock their potential. With a modern take on ancient practices, Dandapani creates an empowering experience for many.

www.dandapani.org

Lumosity:

This tool challenges your brain with games designed to exercise memory and attention. The program is customized to train your brain in a personalized way.

www.lumosity.com

BOOKS WE LOVE:

Above The Line (Steve Satterwhite):

The book helps entrepreneurs and leaders facing the issues of hiring and inspiring employees to carry out your vision.

All Marketers Tell Stories (Seth Godin):

In a retitling of his book, "All Marketers Are Liars", Seth Godin re-emphasizes the importance of telling the truth when telling your company stories.

Creativity Inc (Ed Catmull):

This management book focuses on creativity in business by looking at Pixar Animation Studios.

Double Double (Cameron Herold):

The book describes how to enjoy the "rollercoaster ride of growth" and also how to double the size of your company in three years or less.

The E Myth (Michael E. Gerber):

This book series focuses on entrepreneurship and how to work on your business rather than work in your business.

The 4 Essentials of Entrepreneurial Thinking: What Successful People Didn't Learn in School (Cliff Michaels):

Education activist, Cliff Michaels, calls on his experiences as an entrepreneur to share lessons for success provided by legendary leaders.

Free the Idea Monkey (Mike Maddock):

This book encourages channeling innovative thinking to achieve your most aggressive goals.

Good to Great (Jim Collins):

This book provides a retrospective of the characteristics that propelled certain companies from "good to great" while comparable companies with similar opportunities failed to make the jump.

Launch (Scott Duffy):

This book offers an approach for turning your big ideas into business by focusing on the 90 days immediately before, during, and after starting your business.

Likable Social Media (Dave Kerpen):

This book shares how to use the power of word-of-mouth marketing to transform your business.

Made to Stick (Chip Heath and Dan Heath):

This book examines why some ideas succeed while others fail.

Orbiting the Giant Hairball (Gordon MacKenzie):

In this book, Gordon MacKenzie shares his professional experiences to explain how creativity and the bottom line connect.

Paper Napkin Wisdom (Govindh Jayaraman and Jack Daly):

The book shares five steps to life and business success.

The Power of Habit (Charles Duhigg):

This book examines how successful people achieve success by focusing on patterns that affect every part of our lives.

Purple Cow (Seth Godin):

This book explores how to transform your business by being remarkable.

Scale Up (Verne Harnish):

This book shares tools and techniques for building a dominating business. By focusing on four major decision areas, People, Strategy, Execution and Cash, this book shows business leaders how to get their organizations moving in sync.

Simple Numbers (Greg Crabtree):

Take the mystery out of small business finance with this no-frills guide to understanding the numbers that will guide your business out of any financial black hole.

Start With WHY (Simon Sinek):

This book shares the reasons why some leaders and organizations are more successful and are able to repeat this success over and over.

Steve Jobs (Walter Isaacson):

This biography of Steve Jobs offers a inside look into the creative entrepreneur's revolutionary impact on six industries.

StrengthsFinder 2.0 (Tom Rath):

This book offers a improved assessment of discovering your strengths and developing them in order to succeed every day.

The Tipping Point (Malcolm Gladwell):

This book focuses on how little actions have big effects in business by exploring the tipping point phenomenon.

True North (Bill George):

This book provides a program for finding your True North and leadership success.

The WHY Engine:

This book offers tools to discover your WHY and create messaging around it to improve your organization.

Zombies Ate My Business (Jamie Gerdsen):

This book defines zombies (unproductive employees) and their effect on your company growth and the bottom line.

REMINDER: TO BE MORE, BE MORE OF YOU AND NOT ANYONE ELSE. IN TODAY'S WORLD, IT'S THE SUREST PATH TO STANDING OUT, TAKING OFF AND STAYING ON COURSE.

ABOUT THE AUTHORS

Winnie Brignac Hart (on the left), and Lorrie Brignac Lee (on the right), bring 25+ years of marketing experience, 125+ industry awards and a passion for leveraging their twin talents to help companies translate traditional marketing channels into forward-thinking solutions. They have built a reputation as inspired, award-winning designers and savvy interpreters of business brand and personality. At TwinEngine, they have collaborated with the largest public and privately held corporations in the region, helping them define their distinct advantage and what makes them stand out. They define their business style as collaborative and relationship-based, and bring a right-brain approach to the visual organization of ideas and the left-brain efficiencies of real-time brand management.

The inspiration for TwinEngine: "When we were 11 our dad bought a 4 seater, twin engine plane. It was his lifelong dream to fly. It all started with building small model airplanes, where we watched our brother and Dad fly planes, crash planes, then fix planes. This venture evolved into passenger plane flying lessons – Dad spent countless hours in flight training. It took years and we still remember looking up from our front yard to watch Dad's first fly over one late summer afternoon. We dedicate our mission of helping brands stand out to our Dad, Henry 'Brig' Brignac, who inspires and teaches us that anything is possible – you've got to learn to fly small planes before you can fly the big ones." Thank you, Dad.

THANK YOU

There are so many people to thank that supported us in developing brand traffic control and writing this book. Thank you for the impact you've had on our lives and in our business. Shout out to William Guion and Marcelle Rayner for their relentless pursuit in bringing *Stand Out* to life. To the entire TwinEngine team — you've earned your wings! **Thank you.**

Adam Brackman

Adrienne Palmer

Aimee Siegel

Alex Calicchia

Baird Craft

Barbara McKnight

Becca Armstrong

Billy and Ann Harrison

Brandon Aames

Cameron Herold

Charles Unfried

Christina Harbridge

Clint Greenleaf

Dave Galbenski

Dave Kerpen

Elizabeth Dukes

Elke Laughlin

Erick Slabaugh

Erin Weed

Evan Rudowski

Fran Biderman-Gross

Gary Sanchez

George and Clare Hart

Govindh Jayaraman

Greg Crabtree

Henry Brignac, Jr.

Inga Smith

James Hart

Jaime Gersden

Jamie Douraghy

Jason Jacobs

Joe Kelly

Joel Goldstein

Judy Brignac

Karen Simon

Kevin Briley

Kevin Langley

Lesley Hayes

Linda Dennery

Lisa Roth

Lori Ames

Mahmood Al-Yousif

Marcelle Rayner

Marshall Lee

Mark Martin

Marsha Ralls

Mike Kantrow, Sr.

Mike Maddock

Mike Sparkman

Miranda Lee

Morgan Lee

Natalia Matveeva

Olivia Hart

Paula Manning

Pete Patterson

Ridgely Goldsborough

Rob Simons

Robert Wagnon

Roger Bailey

Ron and Mary Neal

Sandra Jonas Desguin

Scott Offerdaul

Skip Bertman

Steve Satterwhite

Sue Hrib

Susan Lindner

Tommy Brignac

Virginia Miller

Warren Rustand

William Guion

+ many we've missed!